Gradle Essentials

Master the fundamentals of Gradle with this quick and easy-to-read guide

Kunal Dabir

Abhinandan

[PACKT] open source *
PUBLISHING   community experience distilled

BIRMINGHAM - MUMBAI

Gradle Essentials

Copyright © 2015 Packt Publishing

All rights reserved. No part of this book may be reproduced, stored in a retrieval system, or transmitted in any form or by any means, without the prior written permission of the publisher, except in the case of brief quotations embedded in critical articles or reviews.

Every effort has been made in the preparation of this book to ensure the accuracy of the information presented. However, the information contained in this book is sold without warranty, either express or implied. Neither the authors, nor Packt Publishing, and its dealers and distributors will be held liable for any damages caused or alleged to be caused directly or indirectly by this book.

Packt Publishing has endeavored to provide trademark information about all of the companies and products mentioned in this book by the appropriate use of capitals. However, Packt Publishing cannot guarantee the accuracy of this information.

First published: December 2015

Production reference: 1161215

Published by Packt Publishing Ltd.
Livery Place
35 Livery Street
Birmingham B3 2PB, UK.

ISBN 978-1-78398-236-3

www.packtpub.com

Credits

Authors
Kunal Dabir
Abhinandan

Reviewers
Eric Berry
André Burgaud
Michał Huniewicz
Fredrik Sandell

Commissioning Editor
Amarabha Banerjee

Acquisition Editors
Richard Brookes-Bland
Larissa Pinto

Content Development Editor
Rashmi Suvarna

Technical Editor
Madhunikita Sunil Chindarkar

Copy Editor
Trishya Hajare

Project Coordinator
Izzat Contractor

Proofreader
Safis Editing

Indexer
Hemangini Bari

Production Coordinator
Shantanu N. Zagade

Cover Work
Shantanu N. Zagade

About the Authors

Kunal Dabir has over 10 years of experience working with clients ranging from Fortune 500 companies to startups. Currently, he works as a Lead Consultant at ThoughtWorks. He is a Java user group's co-organizer and speaks at various meet-ups and conferences.

While he is always eager to learn a new language, he usually codes in languages such as Groovy, Scala, JavaScript, CoffeeScript, Ruby, and Java. He frequently contributes to open source projects and also hosts his own projects on GitHub.

He has always been passionate about automating and scripting. From there, he got a knack for build tools. Apart from Gradle, he has spent a fair amount of time writing build scripts with tools such as Ant, Maven, Grunt, and Gulp. He was introduced to Gradle in 2011 while using Gaelyk. Since then, Gradle has become his tool of choice for build automation.

He can be found on Twitter and GitHub as `@kdabir`.

Acknowledgments

First and foremost, a big thanks to my loving wife, Smita, and adorable son, Nairit. Both of them patiently tolerated me spending countless hours in front of my Mac and never complained. I would like to thank my parents for always doing everything that they could so that I could do what I like. I dedicate this book to Smita, Nairit, Aai, and Baba.

This book would not have been possible without Packt's trust in me. I would like to thank the editors and coordinators from Packt, including Richard, Parita, Priyanka, Rashmi, Madhunikita, and many more. I would also like to thank Abhinandan for providing a helping hand with the project at the time it was required the most. Also, heartfelt thanks to all the reviewers, André Burgaud, Eric Berry, Fredrik Sandell, and Michał Huniewicz, for painstakingly reviewing all the chapters and providing detailed feedback.

I am grateful to ThoughtWorks for being such an amazing place where I learned so many things.

Last but not the least, this acknowledgement can not be complete without thanking the folks who made Gradle so awesome, those who built and maintained Groovy, and the Groovy community. Kudos to all for the hard work.

Abhinandan is a Java guy with an extensive experience in software design, architecture, and deployment and automation frameworks. He is passionate about providing solutions for different business needs. His other passions include hiking, reading, and travelling. You can contact him at designationtraveller@yahoo.com.

Like how a film cannot be made with just actors and directors—it requires lots of different team members' help, who support at different stages until the movie gets released— a book can't be written with just the effort of one person or the author. It requires lots of support from different people at different stages, without which it would not be possible to put the thoughts on paper and make it available to the audience.

> First and foremost, I would like to thank my family for all the support they gave me throughout this book. They never complained about the weekends and vacations that I compromised while working on this book.
>
> I would like to express my gratitude to the Packt Publishing team (Parita, Purav, and Rashmi), who provided support from the initiation of the idea until the publication of the book. I appreciate that they believed in me and provided me the opportunity to become the co-author of this book.
>
> I would like to thank the reviewers who helped me to improve the quality of this book.
>
> Thanks to Mainak for the quality input and comments, which helped to complete this book. I could not have done it without you.

About the Reviewers

Eric Berry is the co-founder and vice president of engineering at Keeply Inc. He graduated in 2003 from Cal Poly Pomona with a BS in computer science, and has more than 11 years of full-stack development experience working for Evite (http://www.evite.com/), eHarmony (http://www.eharmony.com/), and Chegg (http://www.chegg.com/). He was first introduced to Gradle in late 2010 while working at eHarmony, and created Chegg's middle-tier SOA using Gradle for all Java-based projects. As a supporter of open source software, he's the plugin release manager for the jEdit text editor and also the original author of the Gradle-release and Gradle-templates plugins.

He has worked as a senior software engineer at Evite specializing in full-stack, JSP, Servlet, Spring Framework, Hibernate, "web-2.0" JavaScript based frontend.

He has also worked as a senior software engineer at eHarmony specializing in full-stack, Java, Spring, Struts, Groovy, Spring Integration, Jersey.

He has worked as a lead software engineer at Chegg specializing in backend services, Java, Spring, Hibernate, Gradle, Jersey.

André Burgaud is a software engineer who is passionate about new technologies, programming languages in general, and Python in particular.

He started in law enforcement where he built up an interest in security. A career change led him to join the telecommunication department of the Gendarmerie headquarters in France; later, he implemented network management systems for Qwest broadband services in Minnesota, USA. He currently leads a software development department at Infinite Campus, focusing on the infrastructure for complex web applications.

During his spare time, he attempts to quench his thirst for technology by exploring programming languages, tools, operating systems, servers, or cloud services; also, he likes attending local meetups or online classes, listening to podcasts, and reading books.

Michał Huniewicz is a London-based professional software developer, amateur photo journalist, and one-time dervish. Currently, he is shifting his focus to big data challenges and has been involved in projects across a variety of industries, including banking, media, finance, telecoms, and government. He was also the head developer of an award-winning community portal. He holds an MSc degree in computer science from Adam Mickiewicz University. Learn more about him at `http://www.m1key.me/`.

He has also reviewed *Gradle Effective Implementation Guide* from *Packt Publishing*.

> I would like to thank my friend, Bianca, for being such an amazing inspiration over the years — dziękuję.

Fredrik Sandell is a full-stack software developer with many years of experience developing Java-based web applications. He holds a MSc degree in networks and distributed systems from the Chalmers University of Technology and is currently based in Stockholm, Sweden.

Fredrik is employed at a fantastic company called Squeed AB.

www.PacktPub.com

Support files, eBooks, discount offers, and more

For support files and downloads related to your book, please visit www.PacktPub.com.

Did you know that Packt offers eBook versions of every book published, with PDF and ePub files available? You can upgrade to the eBook version at www.PacktPub.com and as a print book customer, you are entitled to a discount on the eBook copy. Get in touch with us at service@packtpub.com for more details.

At www.PacktPub.com, you can also read a collection of free technical articles, sign up for a range of free newsletters and receive exclusive discounts and offers on Packt books and eBooks.

PACKTLIB

https://www2.packtpub.com/books/subscription/packtlib

Do you need instant solutions to your IT questions? PacktLib is Packt's online digital book library. Here, you can search, access, and read Packt's entire library of books.

Why subscribe?

- Fully searchable across every book published by Packt
- Copy and paste, print, and bookmark content
- On demand and accessible via a web browser

Free access for Packt account holders

If you have an account with Packt at www.PacktPub.com, you can use this to access PacktLib today and view 9 entirely free books. Simply use your login credentials for immediate access.

Table of Contents

Preface	**v**
Chapter 1: Running Your First Gradle Task	**1**
Installing Gradle	**2**
Installing manually	3
Installing on Mac OS X and Linux	3
Installing on Windows	4
Alternate methods of installing Gradle	5
Installing via OS-specific package managers	6
Installing via SDKMAN	6
Verifying the installation	7
Setting JVM options	7
The Gradle command-line interface	**8**
The first Gradle build script	**11**
Task name abbreviation	12
Gradle Daemon	13
Gradle Wrapper	14
Generating wrapper files	14
Running a build via wrapper	14
Summary	**15**
Chapter 2: Building Java Projects	**17**
Building a simple Java project	**17**
Creating a build file	18
Adding source files	18
Building the project	19
A brief introduction to plugins	22
Unit testing	**23**
Adding a unit test source	23
Adding the JUnit to the classpath	24
Running the test	25

Viewing test reports	26
Fitting tests in the workflow	28
Bundling an application distributable	**30**
Running the application with Gradle	32
Building the distribution archive	33
Generating IDE project files	**35**
Summary	**36**
Chapter 3: Building a Web Application	**37**
Building a simple Java web project	**37**
Creating source files	38
Creating a build file	41
Building the artifact	42
Running the web application	44
Plugins to the rescue	45
References	**47**
Project dependencies	**48**
External libraries	48
The dynamic version	49
Transitive dependencies	50
Dependency configurations	51
Repositories	53
Summary	**54**
Chapter 4: Demystifying Build Scripts	**55**
Groovy for Gradle build scripts	**56**
Why Groovy?	56
Groovy primer	57
Running Groovy code	57
Variables	58
Data structures	62
Methods	64
Classes	67
Another look at applying plugins	69
Gradle – an object-oriented build tool	**70**
Build phases	**71**
Initialization	71
Configuration	71
Execution	72
Life cycle callbacks	73
Gradle project API	**73**
Project methods	74
Project properties	74
Extra properties on a project	76

Tasks	**77**
Attaching actions to a task	78
Task flow control	78
dependsOn	79
finalizedBy	79
onlyIf	79
mustRunAfter and shouldRunAfter	80
Creating tasks dynamically	80
Setting default tasks	81
Task types	81
Using task types	82
Creating task types	82
References	**84**
Groovy	84
Gradle API and DSL used in this chapter	84
Summary	**85**
Chapter 5: Multiprojects Build	**87**
The multiproject directory layout	**87**
The settings.gradle file	**89**
Organizing build logic in multiproject builds	**91**
Applying a build logic to all projects	92
Applying build logic to subprojects	95
Dependency on subprojects	96
Summary	**98**
Chapter 6: The Real-world Project with Gradle	**99**
Migrating from an Ant-based project	**99**
Importing an Ant file	100
Using AntBuilder API	101
Rewriting Ant tasks to Gradle tasks	102
Migrating from a Maven project	**103**
Publishing artifacts	**106**
Continuous Integration	**108**
Generating documentation	**111**
Summary	**113**
Chapter 7: Testing and Reporting with Gradle	**115**
Testing with TestNG	**115**
Integration testing	**119**
Code coverage	**121**
Code analysis reports	**124**
Summary	**128**

Chapter 8: Organizing Build Logic and Plugins — 129
- Extracting build logic to buildSrc — 129
- The first plugin — 133
- Configuring plugins — 136
- Summary — 137

Chapter 9: Polyglot Projects — 139
- The polyglot application — 140
- Building Groovy projects — 140
- Building Scala projects — 144
- Joint compilation — 147
- References — 147
- Summary — 147

Index — 149

Preface

When I first came across Gradle in 2011, it was a young yet powerful tool. If I remember correctly, the version was 0.9. It was difficult for me to get started despite Gradle having an adequate official documentation. What I missed the most was a guide that would just help me understand the core concepts first, without having to go through the entire documentation.

Gradle is a fantastic build tool. There is so much to learn about it that new users are often clueless about where to start. It is unwise to expect an application developer to go through the entire Gradle reference material just to understand the basics.

This book attempts to help a reader get started with Gradle by revealing the key concepts in a step-by-step manner. It introduces a more advanced topic succinctly. This book focuses on the practical usage of Gradle that a reader can immediately put to use on his or her project. This book strives to stay true to the spirit of 'essentials' by avoiding going into every possible feature and option that Gradle has to offer. Code samples for applications have been consciously kept very small in order to avoid distractions from application logic.

This book is a quick start guide for Gradle. If you are a Java developer already building your code with Ant or Maven and want to switch to Gradle, this book helps you to quickly understand the different concepts of Gradle. Even if you do not have exposure to other build tools such as Ant or Maven, you can start afresh on Gradle with the help of this book. It starts with the basics of Gradle and then gently moves to concepts such as multimodule projects, migration strategies, testing strategies, Continuous Integration, and code coverage with the help of Gradle.

Preface

What this book covers

This book can be roughly divided into three parts.

Section 1 includes *Chapter 1, Running Your First Gradle Task*, *Chapter 2, Building Java Projects*, and *Chapter 3, Building a Web Application*. This section introduces the basics of Gradle, with very simple examples, which helps readers to create build files for Java projects and Web applications. It gives a gentle start without involving any complex concepts.

Section 2 includes *Chapter 4, Demystifying Build Scripts*, and *Chapter 5, Multiprojects Build*. This section helps the reader to understand the underpinning of Gradle in more depth, still maintaining the 'essentials' aspect of this book. It also helps the reader to understand how to interpret and write scripts that conform to Gradle DSL.

Section 3 includes *Chapter 6*, The *Real-world Project with Gradle*, *Chapter 7, Testing and Reporting with Gradle*, *Chapter 8, Organizing Build Logic and Plugins*, and *Chapter 9, Polyglot Projects*. This section covers more real-world use cases that Gradle users come across. Some examples include migrating to Gradle from the existing build system, using Gradle on CI servers, maintaining code quality with Gradle, using Gradle to build project languages such as Groovy and Scala, and so on. These concepts mostly revolve around what various plugins have to offer and also allows the reader to create their own custom plugins.

Also, there are multiple places in all chapters where the reader can find tips, references, and other informative notes.

Chapter 1, Running Your First Gradle Task, starts with an introduction to Gradle and its installation, subsequently moving on to exploring the Gradle command-line interface, and finally running the first build file.

Chapter 2, Building Java Projects, explains topics such as building Java applications and libraries, unit testing with JUnit, reading test reports, and creating application distributions.

Chapter 3, Building a Web Application, deals with building and running Web applications. It also briefly introduces concepts such as dependencies, repositories, and configurations.

Chapter 4, Demystifying Build Scripts, starts with a primer to the Groovy syntax in the context of Gradle DSL. Then, it goes on to explain the backbone concepts of a Gradle build such as build phases, project API, and various topics related to Gradle tasks.

Chapter 5, Multiprojects Build, covers a few options to structure multiproject directories. Then, covers organization of a build logic, which is a multiproject build.

Chapter 6, The Real-world Project with Gradle, deals with one of the important problems faced by developers, that is, migrating their existing Ant and Maven scripts to Gradle. This chapter provides different strategies and examples, which guide developers to perform migration in a more simpler and manageable way. This chapter also gives an insight into the different ways of publishing artifacts with the help of Gradle and also how a developer can integrate Gradle with Continuous Integration workflow.

Chapter 7, Testing and Reporting with Gradle, deals with the integration of the TestNG framework with Gradle. Apart from unit testing with TestNG, it also deals with different strategies for integration testing, which the user can follow to execute integration tests separate from unit test cases. It also discusses about integrating Sonar with Gradle, which helps developers to analyze the quality of code on different parameters, and JaCoCo integration for code coverage analysis.

Chapter 8, Organizing Build Logic and Plugins, discusses one of the important building blocks of Gradle plugins, without which you will find this book incomplete. It discusses the needs of the plugin and the different ways in which developers can create a plugin based on the project size and complexities.

Chapter 9, Polyglot Projects, demonstrates how to use Gradle for projects that use languages apart from or in addition to Java; this chapter shows the examples of building Groovy and Scala projects.

What you need for this book

Your system must have the following software before executing the code mentioned in the book:

- Gradle
- Java 1.7 or above

For chapters 6-8, you need the following softwares:

- Jenkins
- Ant 1.9.4
- Maven 3.2.2

Who this book is for

This book is for Java and other JVM-based language developers who want to use Gradle or who are already using Gradle on their projects.

No prior knowledge of Gradle is required, but some familiarity with build-related terminologies and an understanding of the Java language would help.

Conventions

In this book, you will find a number of text styles that distinguish between different kinds of information. Here are some examples of these styles and an explanation of their meaning.

Code words in text, database table names, folder names, filenames, file extensions, pathnames, dummy URLs, user input, and Twitter handles are shown as follows: "This class exposes just one method called greet which we can use to generate a greeting message."

A block of code is set as follows:

```
task helloWorld << {
  println "Hello, World!"
}
```

Any command-line input or output is written as follows:

```
$ gradle --version
```

Or it may be written as follows:

```
> gradle --version
```

Whenever some output or code block is truncated it is denoted by an ellipsis (...) like this:

```
$ gradle tasks
...
Other tasks
-----------
helloWorld
...
```

New terms and **important words** are shown in bold. Words that you see on the screen, for example, in menus or dialog boxes, appear in the text like this: "Once the **Submit** button is pressed, we'll get the desired result."

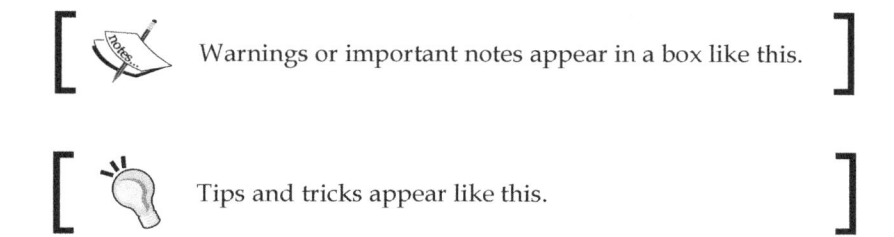

> Warnings or important notes appear in a box like this.

> Tips and tricks appear like this.

Reader feedback

Feedback from our readers is always welcome. Let us know what you think about this book—what you liked or disliked. Reader feedback is important for us as it helps us develop titles that you will really get the most out of.

To send us general feedback, simply e-mail `feedback@packtpub.com`, and mention the book's title in the subject of your message.

If there is a topic that you have expertise in and you are interested in either writing or contributing to a book, see our author guide at `www.packtpub.com/authors`.

Customer support

Now that you are the proud owner of a Packt book, we have a number of things to help you to get the most from your purchase.

Downloading the example code

You can download the example code files from your account at `http://www.packtpub.com` for all the Packt Publishing books you have purchased. If you purchased this book elsewhere, you can visit `http://www.packtpub.com/support` and register to have the files e-mailed directly to you.

Errata

Although we have taken every care to ensure the accuracy of our content, mistakes do happen. If you find a mistake in one of our books—maybe a mistake in the text or the code—we would be grateful if you could report this to us. By doing so, you can save other readers from frustration and help us improve subsequent versions of this book. If you find any errata, please report them by visiting http://www.packtpub.com/submit-errata, selecting your book, clicking on the **Errata Submission Form** link, and entering the details of your errata. Once your errata are verified, your submission will be accepted and the errata will be uploaded to our website or added to any list of existing errata under the Errata section of that title.

To view the previously submitted errata, go to https://www.packtpub.com/books/content/support and enter the name of the book in the search field. The required information will appear under the **Errata** section.

Piracy

Piracy of copyrighted material on the Internet is an ongoing problem across all media. At Packt, we take the protection of our copyright and licenses very seriously. If you come across any illegal copies of our works in any form on the Internet, please provide us with the location address or website name immediately so that we can pursue a remedy.

Please contact us at copyright@packtpub.com with a link to the suspected pirated material.

We appreciate your help in protecting our authors and our ability to bring you valuable content.

Questions

If you have a problem with any aspect of this book, you can contact us at questions@packtpub.com, and we will do our best to address the problem.

Running Your First Gradle Task

We are embarking on a fast-paced ride to learn the *Gradle Essentials*. To take a gentle start, we will first install Gradle. Then, we will get friendly with the Gradle's command-line interface by looking at the usage of the `gradle` command. Also, by the end of this chapter, we would have run our first Gradle build script.

Building a software artifact is a complex process involving various activities such as compiling source code, running automated tests, packaging distributable files, and so on. These activities are further split into many steps, often dependent on the execution order, fetching dependent artifacts, resolving configuration variables, and so on. Executing all these activities manually is cumbersome and often error-prone. A good build automation tool helps us reduce the effort and time it takes to build correct artifacts in a repeatable manner.

Gradle is an advanced build automation tool that brings the best from various proven build tools and innovates on top of them. Gradle can be used to produce artifacts such as web applications, application libraries, documentation, static sites, mobile apps, command lines, and desktop applications. Gradle can be used to build projects based on various languages and technology stacks such as Java, C/C++, Android, Scala, Groovy, Play, Grails, and many more. As **Java Virtual Machine (JVM)** happens to be one of the first class supported platforms by Gradle, the examples in this book will mostly focus on building Java-based projects.

Gradle gives us full control over build just like Ant but without ever needing to repeat ourselves by providing intelligent defaults in the form of conventions. Gradle truly works by conventions over configuration, just like Maven. However, it never gets in our way when we need to deviate. Also this puts it in complete contrast with Maven. Gradle attempts to maintain the right balance between conventions and configurability.

The previous generation of build tools, such as Ant and Maven, chose XML to represent the build logic. While XML is human-readable, it is more of a machine-friendly format (easier to be read/written by programs). It is great for representing and exchanging hierarchical data, but when it comes to writing any logic, even the simplest logic can easily take hundreds of lines. On the other hand, a Gradle build can be configured using very human-friendly Groovy DSL. Groovy is a powerful, expressive, and low ceremony dynamic language and is a perfect fit for build scripts.

Gradle itself is a **JVM** application written in Java and Groovy. Since Gradle runs on the JVM, it runs the same way on Windows, Mac OS X and Linux. Gradle also boasts an advanced dependency resolution system and can resolve dependencies from the existing Maven and Ivy repositories or even a file system.

Over the years Gradle has matured into a very stable open source project with active contributors and commercial backing. The rich plugin ecosystem and vibrant community makes Gradle an excellent choice for a variety of projects. Gradle already has an impressive list of adopters, which includes tech giants such as Google Android, LinkedIn, Unity 3D, Netflix and many more. Open source libraries and frameworks such as Spring, Hibernate, and Grails are using Gradle to power their builds.

Installing Gradle

Before we move forward with running Gradle, we must have it installed on our machine. There are multiple ways through which Gradle can be installed and updated. We will first see a more manual way to install Gradle and then take a quick look at installing it via some commonly used package managers. We can choose any one method that fits the bill. Irrespective of the way we install Gradle, we must meet the following prerequisite.

Gradle needs **Java Runtime Environment (JRE)** 6 or **Java Development Kit (JDK)** 1.6 or higher. There is no other dependency. We recommend having JDK installed. To verify this, on the command line, we can check the Java version with the following command:

```
$ java -version
java version "1.8.0"
Java(TM) SE Runtime Environment (build 1.8.0-b132)
Java HotSpot(TM) 64-Bit Server VM (build 25.0-b70, mixed mode)
```

If we don't see the output more or less like the one shown in the preceding command, there is problem with our JDK installation.

> The latest JDK can be downloaded from the following URL:
> http://www.oracle.com/technetwork/java/javase/downloads/index.html

Installing manually

If we want a finer control over the installation then this is a suitable route. This could be the case, when we cannot use the package managers, want very specific binaries to be downloaded and installed, or behind corporate firewalls where automatic downloading by package managers is not allowed. We need to download the Gradle binaries and make them available for use on the command line.

The latest Gradle distribution can be downloaded from http://www.gradle.org/downloads. As of writing the latest version is 2.9.

Gradle binary distribution comes in two flavors as follows:

- gradle-2.9-all.zip: This contains binaries, sources, and documentation
- gradle-2.9-bin.zip: This contains binaries only

We can download any of the above depending on what we need. Also, this is an OS-independent zip so the same zip can be extracted on Mac OS X, Windows, and Linux. The next section makes the Gradle command available on the command line. This section is dependent on the OS we use.

Installing on Mac OS X and Linux

Let's say we extracted the downloaded zip as ~/gradle-2.9/. Now, we just need to add the following two lines at the end of .bashrc/, .bash_profile/, or .zshrc, depending on the OS and the shell that we use:

```
export GRADLE_HOME=~/gradle-2.9
export PATH=$PATH:$GRADLE_HOME/bin
```

Restart the terminal or source the modified file to have the change take effect.

Installing on Windows

Let's say we extracted the zip as `C:\gradle-2.9`, then perform the following steps:

1. Open the Start menu, right click on **Computer** and select **Properties**.
2. On **Advanced system settings**, select the **Advanced** tab, and then select **Environment Variables...**.

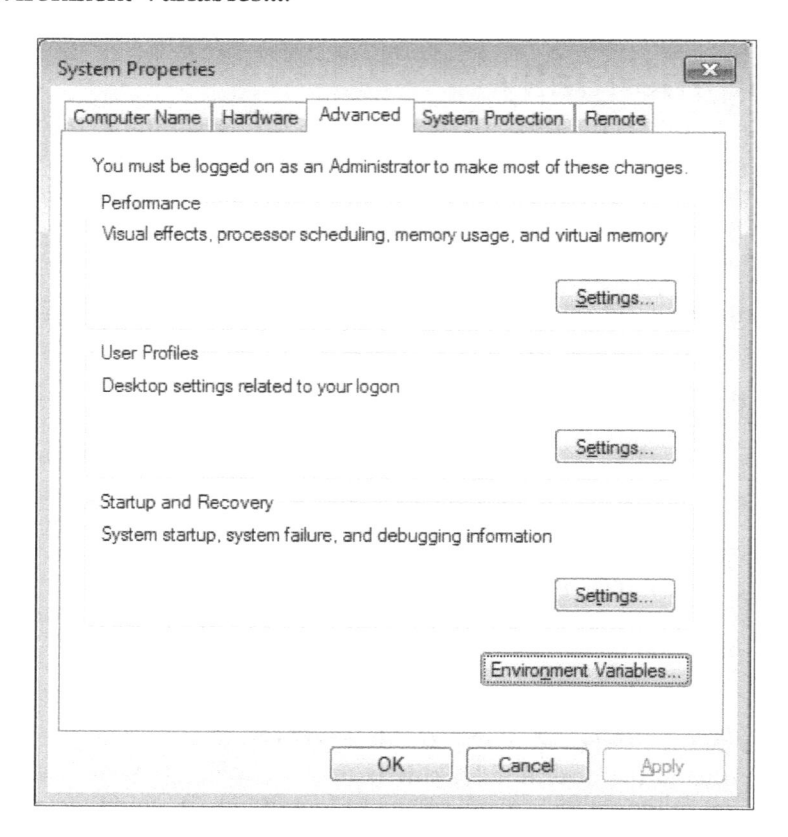

3. Click on **New**.
4. Create a `GRADLE_HOME` environment variable with the value `C:\gradle-2.9`.

> **Downloading the example code**
>
> You can download the example code files from your account at http://www.packtpub.com for all the Packt Publishing books you have purchased. If you purchased this book elsewhere, you can visit http://www.packtpub.com/support and register to have the files e-mailed directly to you.

> In future when we download the later version of Gradle, we would need to change on this value to point to the correct folder.

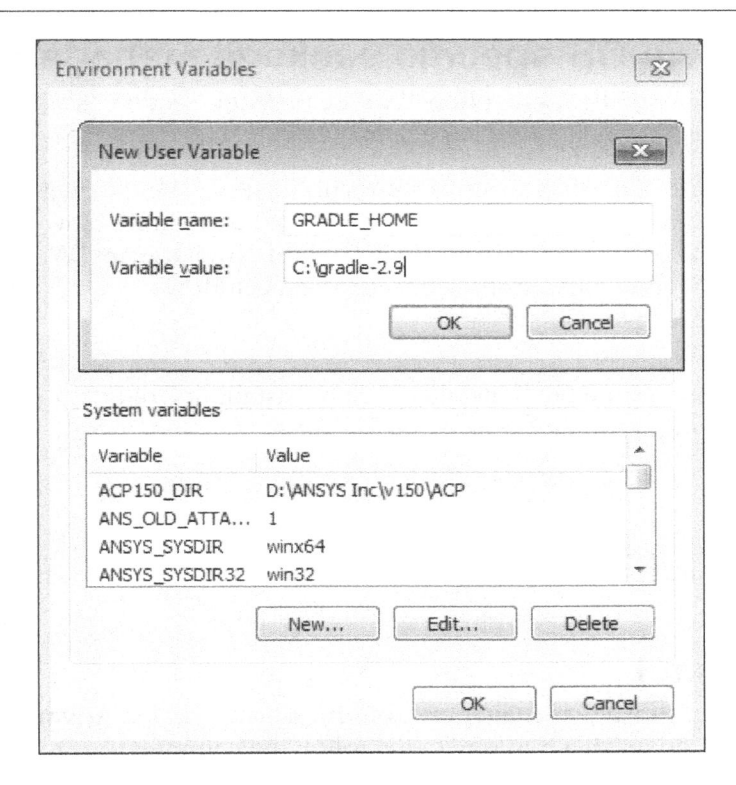

5. Edit (or add if not already there) the `PATH` environment variable. At the end of its value, append `;%GRADLE_HOME%\bin` (add a semicolon if multiple path entries exist).

Alternate methods of installing Gradle

Although the manual installation gives absolute control over the installation process, various tasks such as downloading and extracting the right version, upgrading to the latest versions, uninstalling, and editing environment variables quickly become cumbersome and error-prone. That is why many people prefer package managers to control the whole process.

Installing via OS-specific package managers

While installing manually, as mentioned in the previous section, is very easy, we can make it super-easy by using a package manager.

Some Linux distributions like Ubuntu ship with their package manager, Mac OS X, Windows don't have any package manager installed by default. However, luckily, there are multiple package managers available for both platforms. We will see the example of Homebrew on Mac and Chocolatey on Windows.

Mac OS X

Make sure we have Homebrew installed. If it is, installing Gradle is only a matter of using the following command:

```
$ brew install gradle
```

> More details on Homebrew can be found at http://brew.sh.

Linux (Ubuntu)

Using the built in package manager on Ubuntu, which is called **Advanced Packaging Tool** (**APT**), we can install Gradle with the following command:

```
$ sudo apt-get install gradle
```

Windows

If we have Chocolatey installed, installing Gradle is just a command away:

```
c:\> cinst gradle
```

> More details on Chocolatey can be found at https://chocolatey.org.

Installing via SDKMAN

SDKMAN stands for **the Software Development Kit Manager**. In its own words, the website describes it as: *SDKMAN! is a tool for managing parallel versions of multiple Software Development Kits on most Unix based systems.*

The advantage SDKMAN has over other package managers is that we can have multiple Gradle versions installed on a system and select a different version for a given project. If we have it installed, all we need to do is run following command:

```
$ sdk install gradle
```

SDKMAN can be installed from http://sdkman.io/.

Verifying the installation

In whichever way we choose to install Gradle, it's a good idea to verify that if it's working before we move ahead. We can do this by simply checking for Gradle's version on the command line:

```
$ gradle --version

------------------------------------------------------------
Gradle 2.9
------------------------------------------------------------


Build time:   2015-11-17 07:02:17 UTC
Build number: none
Revision:     b463d7980c40d44c4657dc80025275b84a29e31f

Groovy:       2.4.4
Ant:          Apache Ant(TM) version 1.9.3 compiled on December 23 2013
JVM:          1.8.0_25 (Oracle Corporation 25.25-b02)
OS:           Mac OS X 10.10.5 x86_64
```

If we see output similar to the above, we have Gradle installed correctly on our machine.

> We can use -v instead --version to get the same result.

Setting JVM options

Although it's not required most of the time, but if in case we need to set some global options for the JVM that Gradle will use, Gradle provides us a convenient way to do that. We can set the GRADLE_OPTS environment variable with acceptable flags to tune the JVM.

Gradle also honors the JAVA_OPTS environment variable. However, we need to be careful when setting it, as this affects the setting for all the Java programs on a machine. Setting that we want to keep common for all the Java apps should be done via this variable and those that only need to be applied to Gradle should be set via GRADLE_OPTS.

> Some commonly used options are -Xms and -Xmx, which set the minimum and maximum heap size of the JVM.

The Gradle command-line interface

Gradle, just like other build tools, is primarily run from a command line. That's why it is worth spending some time to get familiar with its command-line interface. Typically, a gradle command is issued from the root of a project directory with some tasks to be executed. Let's say we are in the hello-gradle directory, which is currently empty.

Gradle provides a very simple **command-line interface (CLI)**, which takes the following form:

```
gradle [options...] [tasks...]
```

As we can see, apart from the gradle command itself, everything else is optional. The options tweak the execution of the Gradle whereas tasks, which we will see in detail later, are the basic units of work. Options are common across all projects and are specific to Gradle but tasks may vary depending on the project in which the gradle command is being run.

There are some tasks that are available on all projects. One such task is help:

```
$ gradle help
:help

Welcome to Gradle 2.9.

To run a build, run gradle <task> ...

To see a list of available tasks, run gradle tasks
```

```
To see a list of command-line options, run gradle --help

To see more detail about a task, run gradle help --task <task>

BUILD SUCCESSFUL

Total time: 0.639 secs
```

Gradle is helping us out by telling us how to find all the available tasks and list all command-line options. Let's first check what other tasks are currently available on our project. Remember we are still in the empty directory `hello-gradle`:

```
$ gradle tasks
:tasks


------------------------------------------------------------
All tasks runnable from root project
------------------------------------------------------------

Build Setup tasks
-----------------
init - Initializes a new Gradle build. [incubating]
wrapper - Generates Gradle wrapper files. [incubating]

Help tasks
----------
components - Displays the components produced by root project 'hello-gradle'. [incubating]
dependencies - Displays all dependencies declared in root project 'hello-gradle'.
dependencyInsight - Displays the insight into a specific dependency in root project 'hello-gradle'.
help - Displays a help message.
model - Displays the configuration model of root project 'hello-gradle'. [incubating]
projects - Displays the sub-projects of root project 'hello-gradle'.
properties - Displays the properties of root project 'hello-gradle'.
tasks - Displays the tasks runnable from root project 'hello-gradle'.
```

Running Your First Gradle Task

```
To see all tasks and more detail, run gradle tasks --all

To see more detail about a task, run gradle help --task <task>

BUILD SUCCESSFUL

Total time: 0.652 secs
```

This shows us some generic tasks that are available even without us adding any task to our project. We can try running all these tasks and see the output. We will see these tasks in details in the upcoming chapters.

The other useful command `gradle help` suggested us to check all the available options with the `--help` option.

> The `help` task is not the same as the `--help` option.

When we run the `gradle --help` command, we get the following output:

```
$ gradle --help

USAGE: gradle [option...] [task...]

-?, -h, --help          Shows this help message.
-a, --no-rebuild        Do not rebuild project dependencies.
-b, --build-file        Specifies the build file.
…..
```

(The output is truncated for brevity.)

The option has a long form such as `--help` and may have a short from such as `-h`. We have already used one option before, that is `--version` or `-v`, which prints information about the Gradle version. The following are some commonly used options; there are many more options, which can be seen using the `gradle --help` command:

Options	Description
-b, --build-file	This specifies a build file (default: `build.gradle`)
--continue	This continues task execution even after a task failure
-D, --system-prop	This sets the system property of the JVM

Options	Description
`-d, --debug`	This prints debug level logs
`--gui`	This starts Gradle GUI
`-i, --info`	This prints info level logs
`-P, --project-prop`	This adds a property to the project
`-q, --quiet`	This logs only errors
`-s, --stacktrace`	This prints stack traces for exceptions
`-x, --exclude-task`	This excludes a specific task

The first Gradle build script

So we are now ready to get our feet wet and see our first Gradle script in action. Let's create a file called `build.gradle` in the `hello-gradle` directory. Unless the build file path is provided using the `--build-file` option, Gradle treats the current directory as a project root and tries to find the `build.gradle` file there. If we have used Ant or Maven earlier, we can relate this file with `build.xml` or `pom.xml`, respectively.

Now, open the `build.gradle` file and let's declare a task by adding the following line:

```
task helloWorld
```

We should be able to see this task on the command line as follows:

```
$ gradle tasks
...
Other tasks
-----------
helloWorld
...
```

Here, we have successfully created a task object called `helloWorld`. Tasks are first-class objects in Gradle, which means they have properties and methods on them. This gives us tremendous flexibility in terms of customizability and programmability of build.

However, this task actually does not do anything yet. So let's add some meaningful action to this task:

```
task helloWorld << {
  println "Hello, World!"
}
```

Now from the command line, we can execute this task by issuing the following command:

$ gradle -q helloWorld

Hello, World!

Notice that we used the -q flag to reduce the verbosity in the output. When this task is run, we see the output that our task generates but nothing from Gradle unless it's an error.

Now, let's try to briefly understand the `build.gradle` file. The first line declares the tasks and starts the body of a code block that will be executed at the end. The left shift operator (<<) might feel oddly placed, but it is very important in this context. We will see in the later chapters what it exactly means. The second line is a Groovy statement that prints the given string to the console. Also, the third line ends the code block.

> Groovy's `println "Hello, World!"` is equivalent to `System.out.println("Hello, World!")` in Java.

Task name abbreviation

While calling a gradle task from a command line, we can save a few keystrokes by typing only the characters that are enough to uniquely identify the task name. For example, the task `helloWorld` can be called using `gradle hW`. We can also use `helloW`, `hWorld`, or even `heWo`. However, if we just call `gradle h`, then the `help` task will be called.

This comes very handy when we need to frequently call long Gradle task names. For example, a task named `deployToProductionServer` can be invoked just by calling `gradle dTPS`, provided that this does not match any other task name abbreviation.

Gradle Daemon

While we are talking about frequently calling Gradle, it is a good time to know about a recommended technique to boost the performance of our builds. Gradle Daemon, a process that keeps running in the background, can speed up the builds significantly.

For a given gradle command invocation, we can specify the `--daemon` flag to enable the Daemon process. However, we should keep in mind that when we start the daemon, only the subsequent builds will be faster, but not the current one.
For example:

```
$ gradle helloWorld --daemon
Starting a new Gradle Daemon for this build (subsequent builds will be faster).
:helloWorld
Hello, World!


BUILD SUCCESSFUL

Total time: 2.899 secs
```

```
$ gradle helloWorld
:helloWorld
Hello, World!

BUILD SUCCESSFUL

Total time: 0.6 secs
```

In the preceding example, if we notice the time taken by two runs, the second one completed much faster, thanks to the Gradle Daemon.

We can also prevent a specific build invocation from utilizing a Daemon process by passing the `--no-daemon` flag.

There are various ways to enable or disable Gradle Daemon, which are documented at https://docs.gradle.org/current/userguide/gradle_daemon.html

Gradle Wrapper

A Gradle Wrapper consists of a `gradlew` shell script for Linux/Mac OS X, a `gradlew.bat` batch script for Windows, and a few helper files. These files can be generated by running a gradle `wrapper` task and should be checked into the version control system (VCS) along with project sources. Instead of using the system-wide `gradle` command, we can run the builds via the wrapper script.

Some of the advantages of running builds via a wrapper script are as follows:

1. We don't need to download and install Gradle manually. The wrapper script takes care of this.
2. It uses a specific version of Gradle that the project needs. This reduces the risk of breaking a project's build because of incompatible Gradle versions. We can safely upgrade (or downgrade) the system-wide Gradle installation without affecting our projects.
3. It transparently enforces the same Gradle version for our project across all developers' machines in the team.
4. This is extremely useful in Continuous Integration build environments, as we do not need to install/update Gradle on the servers.

Generating wrapper files

The Gradle `wrapper` task is already available to all Gradle projects. To generate the wrapper scripts and supporting files, just execute the following code from the command line:

```
$ gradle wrapper
```

While generating `wrapper`, we can specify the exact Gradle version as follows:

```
$ gradle wrapper --gradle-version 2.9
```

In this example, we are specifying the Gradle version to be used is 2.9. After running this command, we should check-in the generated files into VCS. We can customize the `wrapper` task to use a configured Gradle version, produce wrapper scripts with different names, change their locations, and so on.

Running a build via wrapper

For availing the benefits of a wrapper script, instead of using the gradle command, we need to call the wrapper script based on our OS.

On Mac OS X/Linux:

```
$ ./gradlew taskName
```

On Windows:

```
$ gradlew taskName
```

We can use the arguments and flags exactly in the same way as we pass to the `gradle` command.

Summary

In this chapter, we started with a brief introduction to Gradle. Then, we looked at manual installation and also installation via package managers. We also learned about Gradle's command-line interface. Also, finally, we wrote our first Gradle build script.

If you have followed the chapter until this point, you are all set to check out any Gradle-based project on your machine and execute builds. Also, you are equipped with the knowledge to write a very basic Gradle build script. Going forward, we will look at building Java-based projects with Gradle.

2
Building Java Projects

In the previous chapter, we saw a very basic build script, which just printed the customary `Hello World` on the console. Now that we are comfortable with the Gradle command line interface, it's a perfect time for us to jump-start our journey with a simple Java project.

In this chapter, we will see how to build and test simple Java projects with Gradle, how external dependencies are added to the classpath, and how building distributable binaries work.

We will try to keep the Java code as minimal as possible so that we can focus more on the build of the project. Along the way, we will learn some best practices that a Gradle-based project should follow. It's okay if we are not able to comprehend all the build script syntax in this chapter because we are going to see that in detail in *Chapter 4, Demystifying Build Scripts*.

Building a simple Java project

To demonstrate the Java project's build with Gradle, let's create a very simple Java application that will greet a user. Just a tad bit more than a `hello world` in terms of application logic.

Firstly, create a directory called `hello-java`. This is our project directory. For the following steps, feel free to choose an IDE/text editor of your choice for editing the files.

Creating a build file

In the root of the project directory, let's create the `build.gradle` file and add the following code line to it:

```
apply plugin: 'java'
```

Yes, that's all that goes into the build file for now, a single line. We will soon see what it means.

Adding source files

By default, like Maven, the Java source files are read from the `src/main/java` directory of the project. We can configure this, of course, but let's save that for later. Let's create this directory structure in our project.

Now, we need to create a Java class that would generate the greeting message. Also, we would create a `Main` class with a `main` method so that an app can be run from a command line. The Java files should be kept in a source root directory under a proper package structure. We will use the `com.packtpub.ge.hello` package for this example:

```
hello-java
├── build.gradle              // build file
└── src
    └── main
        └── java              // source root
            └── com
                └── packtpub
                    └── ge
                        └── hello
                            ├── GreetingService.java
                            └── Main.java
```

As we can see in the preceding structure, we have created the package structure under the `src/main/java` source root.

Let's create the `GreetingService.java` file:

```java
package com.packtpub.ge.hello;

public class GreetingService {
    public String greet(String user) {
        return "Hello " + user;
    }
}
```

This class exposes just one method called `greet`, which we can use to generate a greeting message.

Here is how our `Main.java` looks:

```
package com.packtpub.ge.hello;

public class Main {
    public static void main(String[] args) {
        GreetingService service = new GreetingService();
        System.out.println(service.greet(args[0]));
    }
}
```

This class has a `main` method, which will be invoked when a program is run. It instantiates the `GreetingService` and prints the output of the `greet` method on a console.

Building the project

After adding the Java files, we now want to compile the project and produce the class files. It can be simply done by calling the following task from a command line:

```
$ gradle compileJava
```

The compiled classes go into `build/classes/main` relative to the project root. You can confirm by checking the project tree again. We will ignore other files and directories for now:

```
hello-java
...
├── build
│   ├── classes
│   │   └── main
│   │       └── com
│   │           └── packtpub
│   │               └── ge
│   │                   └── hello
│   │                       ├── GreetingService.class
│   │                       └── Main.class
...
```

Building Java Projects

At this point, we can directly run the class, but let's ask for more and generate the .jar file for our application. Let's run the following task:

```
$ gradle build
```

It produces a Jar for our project in the build/libs directory:

```
hello-java
...
├── build
│   ...
│   ├── libs
│   │   └── hello-java.jar
...
```

Let's test if the Jar works as expected. To run the Jar, issue the following command:

```
$ java -cp build/libs/hello-java.jar \
       com.packtpub.ge.hello.Main Reader
```

We are passing the Reader as an argument to our java Main class 's main method. This will produce the following output:

```
Hello Reader
```

> When we run the build task, Gradle also invokes the compileJava and other dependent tasks before actually executing the build task. So, we don't need to explicitly call compileJava here to compile classes.

The name of the .jar file is the same as that of the project. This can be configured by setting the archivesBaseName property in the build.gradle file. For example, to generate the Jar named my-app.jar, add the following code line to the build file:

```
    archivesBaseName = "my-app"
```

Now, let's fire:

```
$ gradle clean
```

Also, check the directory tree again. No surprise, it's cleaned keeping the source files intact.

We know from our experiences with Ant that, even for the project of this size, we would have to define at least a handful of targets and this would be quite a few lines of XML. While Maven would have worked by convention, still the Maven's `pom.xml` needs some ceremony before it's even a valid `pom.xml` file. So, a minimal `pom.xml` file would still look like five to six lines of XML.

Compare that with the simplicity and carefully chosen sensible defaults by Gradle.

This is a good point where we should see what all tasks were brought into our build by the `java` plugin:

```
$ gradle -q tasks
------------------------------------------------------------
All tasks runnable from root project
------------------------------------------------------------

Build tasks
-----------
assemble - Assembles the outputs of this project.
build - Assembles and tests this project.
buildDependents - Assembles and tests this project and all projects that depend on it.
buildNeeded - Assembles and tests this project and all projects it depends on.
classes - Assembles main classes.
clean - Deletes the build directory.
jar - Assembles a jar archive containing the main classes.
testClasses - Assembles test classes.

Build Setup tasks
-----------------
init - Initializes a new Gradle build. [incubating]
```

```
wrapper - Generates Gradle wrapper files. [incubating]

Documentation tasks
-------------------
javadoc - Generates Javadoc API documentation for the main source code.
Help tasks
----------
components - Displays the components produced by root project 'hello-
java'. [incubating]
dependencies - Displays all dependencies declared in root project 'hello-
java'.
dependencyInsight - Displays the insight into a specific dependency in
root project 'hello-java'.
help - Displays a help message.
model - Displays the configuration model of root project 'hello-java'.
[incubating]
projects - Displays the sub-projects of root project 'hello-java'.
properties - Displays the properties of root project 'hello-java'.
tasks - Displays the tasks runnable from root project 'hello-java'.

Verification tasks
------------------
check - Runs all checks.
test - Runs the unit tests.
...
```

It is interesting to see so many useful tasks available on our build by merely applying the `java` plugin. Clearly, Gradle employs a very powerful plugin mechanism that can be leveraged to apply the **don't repeat yourself** (**DRY**) principle on build logic.

A brief introduction to plugins

Gradle by itself is nothing more than a task runner. It does not know how to compile a Java file or where to read the source files. It means that these tasks are not there by default. As we saw in the last chapter, a Gradle build file, without any plugin applied, contained very few tasks.

A plugin adds relevant tasks and conventions to a Gradle build. In our current example, all the tasks such as `compileJava`, `build`, `clean`, and many more are essentially brought in by the `java` plugin that we applied to our build.

This means, Gradle does not force us to use a particular way to compile a Java project. It's completely up to us to choose the `java` plugin for our build. We can configure it to suit our needs. If we still don't like the way it works, we are free to add our own tasks directly to the build or through a custom plugin that will work the way we want.

There are number of plugins that come out of the box with Gradle. The `java` plugin is one such plugin. Throughout the course of this book, we will see many such plugins, which will bring in a lot of interesting functionality to our build.

Unit testing

Unit testing is an indispensable aspect of software development. Testing gives us confidence that our code works fine and provides us a safety net when refactoring. Fortunately, Gradle's Java plugin makes it simple and easy to unit test your code.

We will write a simple test for the same example app we created above. We will create our first unit test now using JUnit (v4.12) library.

> More information about JUnit can be found at `http://junit.org`.

Adding a unit test source

Again, like Maven, Java test sources are kept in the `src/test/java` directory relative to the project root. We will create this directory and, as a good practice, the test package structure will reflect the same hierarchy as the source packages.

```
...
src
└── test
    └── java          // test source root
        └── com
            └── packtpub
                └── ge
                    └── hello
                        └── GreetingServiceTest.java
...
```

We will add test for the `GreetingService`. By convention, the name of test will be `GreetingServiceTest.java`. The following is the code of this file:

```
package com.packtpub.ge.hello;

import org.junit.Before;
import org.junit.Test;
import static org.junit.Assert.assertEquals;

public class GreetingServiceTest {

    GreetingService service;

    @Before
    public void setup() {
        service = new GreetingService();
    }

    @Test
    public void testGreet() {
        assertEquals("Hello Test", service.greet("Test"));
    }
}
```

The test sets up an instance of **System Under Test (SUT)**, which is `GreetingService`, and the `testGreet` method checks the equality of the SUT's `greet` methods output to get the expected message.

Now, take a moment and try to compile tests by using the `compileTestJava` task, which is exactly the same as `compileJava`, but compiles the test source files. Did it compile just fine? If not, can we take a guess as to what could have gone wrong?

The task should have failed with a bunch of compilation errors because JUnit, which is an external library, was not on the classpath to compile the files.

Adding the JUnit to the classpath

To compile and run this test case, we need JUnit library on the classpath. It is important to remember that this dependency is only required while compiling and running the tests. Our application does not depend on JUnit for its compilation or on runtime. We also need to tell where to search for this artifact so that Gradle can download it if there is a need. To do this, we need to update the `build.gradle` file as follows:

```
apply plugin: 'java'

repositories {
```

```
        mavenCentral()
    }

    dependencies {
        testCompile 'junit:junit:4.12'
    }
```

There are two additions to this build file, from what we already know.

In the `dependencies` section, we list down all the dependencies of the project along with their scope. We declared JUnit to be made available in the `testCompile` scope.

In the `repositories` section, we configure the type and location of the repository where external dependencies will be found. In this example, we tell Gradle to get the dependencies from the Maven central repository. Since Maven central is a very commonly used repo, Gradle provides a shortcut to configure it thorough the `mavenCentral()` method call.

We will cover both the sections in greater depth in the next chapter.

Running the test

We are interested in running the tests to check whether everything is working as expected. Let's run the `test` task, which will also sequentially run all the tasks that the `test` task depends on. We can also verify this by looking at the output that lists all the tasks that have been run as part of this build:

```
$ gradle test
:compileJava
:processResources UP-TO-DATE
:classes
:compileTestJava
:processTestResources UP-TO-DATE
:testClasses
:test

BUILD SUCCESSFUL

Total time: 1.662 secs
```

Building Java Projects

It looks like the tests passed. To see how Gradle tells us when a test fails, let's intentionally change the expected value in assertion to `Test Hello` so that the assertion fails:

```
@Test
public void testGreet() {
    assertEquals("Test Hello", service.greet("Guest"));
}
```

Then run the command again to see the result when the test fails:

```
$ gradle test
:compileJava
:processResources UP-TO-DATE
:classes
:compileTestJava
:processTestResources UP-TO-DATE
:testClasses
:test

com.packtpub.ge.hello.GreetingServiceTest > testGreet FAILED
    org.junit.ComparisonFailure at GreetingServiceTest.java:18
1 test completed, 1 failed
:test FAILED

FAILURE: Build failed with an exception.

......
```

Yes, so the test failed and the output tells you about the file and the line number as well. Also, it points you to the report file, which includes more details of the test failure.

Viewing test reports

Whether the test passes or not, a nice HTML report is created with details of all the tests that are run. By default, this report is located at `build/reports/tests/index.html` relative to the project root. You can open this file in a browser.

For the above failure, the report looks something like this:

Test Summary

1	1	0	0.003s
tests	failures	ignored	duration

0% successful

Failed tests   Packages   Classes

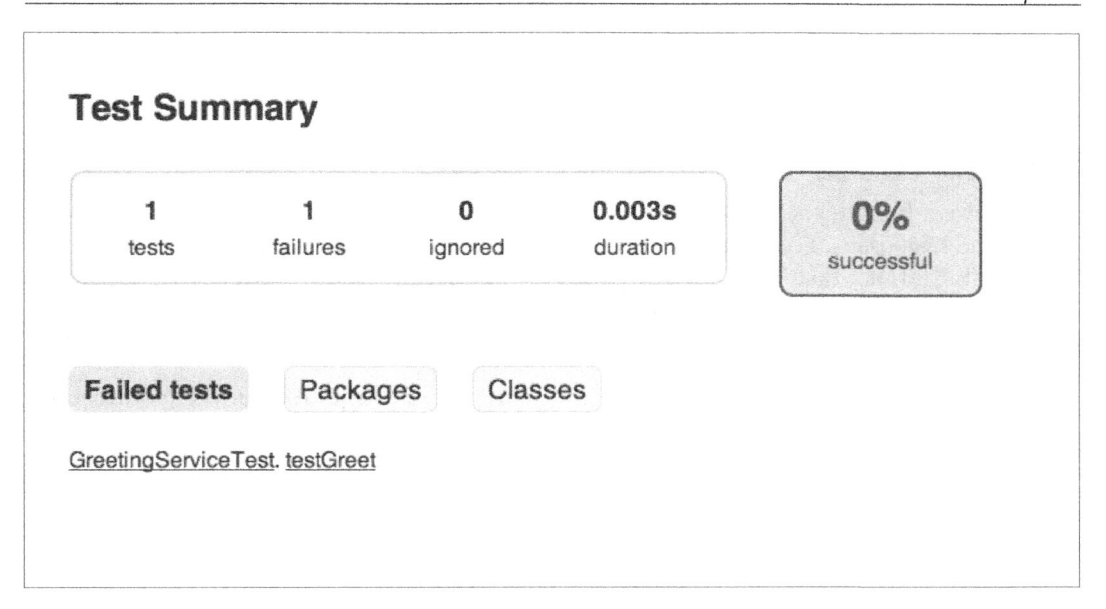

GreetingServiceTest. testGreet

If we click on the failed test, we get to see the details of the failure:

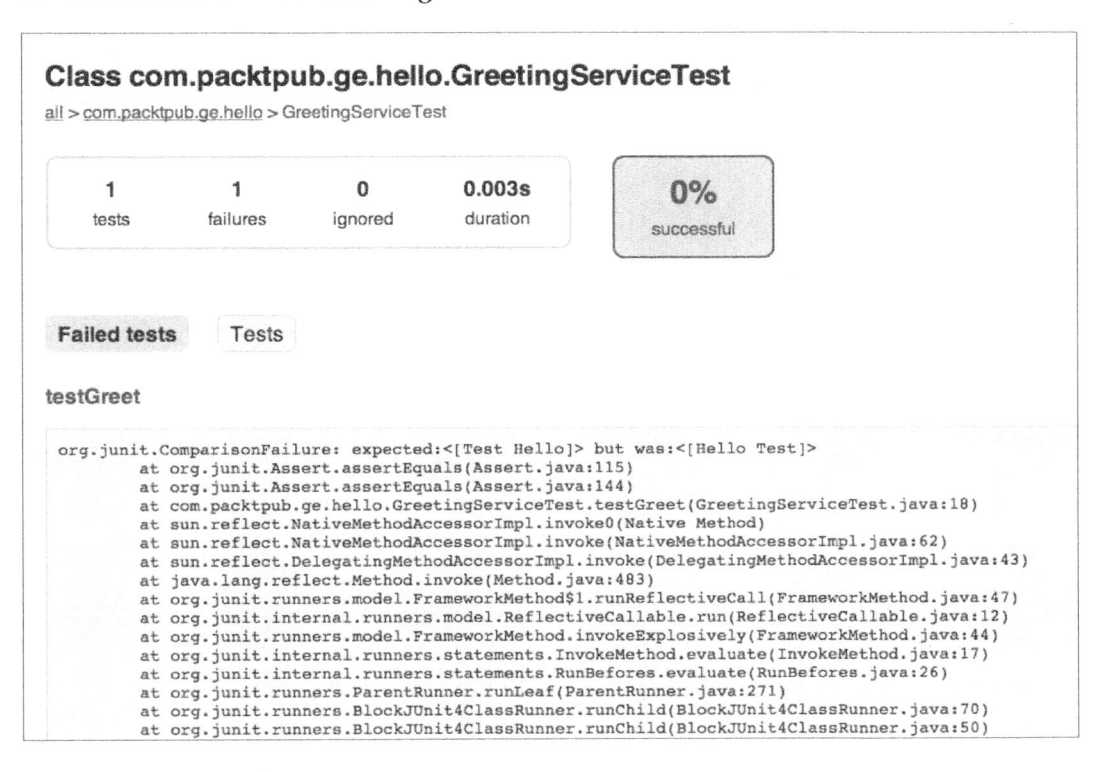

Class com.packtpub.ge.hello.GreetingServiceTest

all > com.packtpub.ge.hello > GreetingServiceTest

1	1	0	0.003s
tests	failures	ignored	duration

0% successful

Failed tests   Tests

testGreet

```
org.junit.ComparisonFailure: expected:<[Test Hello]> but was:<[Hello Test]>
        at org.junit.Assert.assertEquals(Assert.java:115)
        at org.junit.Assert.assertEquals(Assert.java:144)
        at com.packtpub.ge.hello.GreetingServiceTest.testGreet(GreetingServiceTest.java:18)
        at sun.reflect.NativeMethodAccessorImpl.invoke0(Native Method)
        at sun.reflect.NativeMethodAccessorImpl.invoke(NativeMethodAccessorImpl.java:62)
        at sun.reflect.DelegatingMethodAccessorImpl.invoke(DelegatingMethodAccessorImpl.java:43)
        at java.lang.reflect.Method.invoke(Method.java:483)
        at org.junit.runners.model.FrameworkMethod$1.runReflectiveCall(FrameworkMethod.java:47)
        at org.junit.internal.runners.model.ReflectiveCallable.run(ReflectiveCallable.java:12)
        at org.junit.runners.model.FrameworkMethod.invokeExplosively(FrameworkMethod.java:44)
        at org.junit.internal.runners.statements.InvokeMethod.evaluate(InvokeMethod.java:17)
        at org.junit.internal.runners.statements.RunBefores.evaluate(RunBefores.java:26)
        at org.junit.runners.ParentRunner.runLeaf(ParentRunner.java:271)
        at org.junit.runners.BlockJUnit4ClassRunner.runChild(BlockJUnit4ClassRunner.java:70)
        at org.junit.runners.BlockJUnit4ClassRunner.runChild(BlockJUnit4ClassRunner.java:50)
```

We can see `org.junit.ComparisonFailure: expected:<[Test Hello]> but was:<[Hello Test]>` in the first line of the stack trace.

Fitting tests in the workflow

Now that we have tests in place, it makes sense to build our project binaries (.jar) only if the tests pass. For that, we need to define some kind of flow between the tasks such that, if a task fails, the pipeline is broken there and the subsequent tasks are not executed. So, in our examples, the build's execution should depend on the test's success.

Guess what, it has already been taken care by the `java` plugin for us. We just need to call the last task in the flow, and all the tasks that the called tasks depend on will be called sequentially and the build will not succeed if any of the tasks fails.

```
$ gradle build
```

Also, we don't need to call all the tasks that the build depends on explicitly because they will be called anyway.

Now let's fix the test and see the Jar getting created again:

```
$gradle build
:compileJava UP-TO-DATE
:processResources UP-TO-DATE
:classes UP-TO-DATE
:jar UP-TO-DATE
:assemble UP-TO-DATE
:compileTestJava
:processTestResources UP-TO-DATE
:testClasses
:test
:check
:build

BUILD SUCCESSFUL

Total time: 1.617 secs
```

Yay! So the tests have passed and we can build binaries of our app again.

Notice how intelligently Gradle figures out that, if only tests were changed, it compiled only the tests. In the preceding output, `compileJava` shows `UP-TO-DATE`, means nothing was changed and, hence, Gradle didn't unnecessarily compile the source files again.

> If we need to force run task actions even if nothing has changed between the two runs, we can pass the `--rerun-tasks` flag on the command line so that all task actions can run.

If we see the test reports again, they will look as follows:

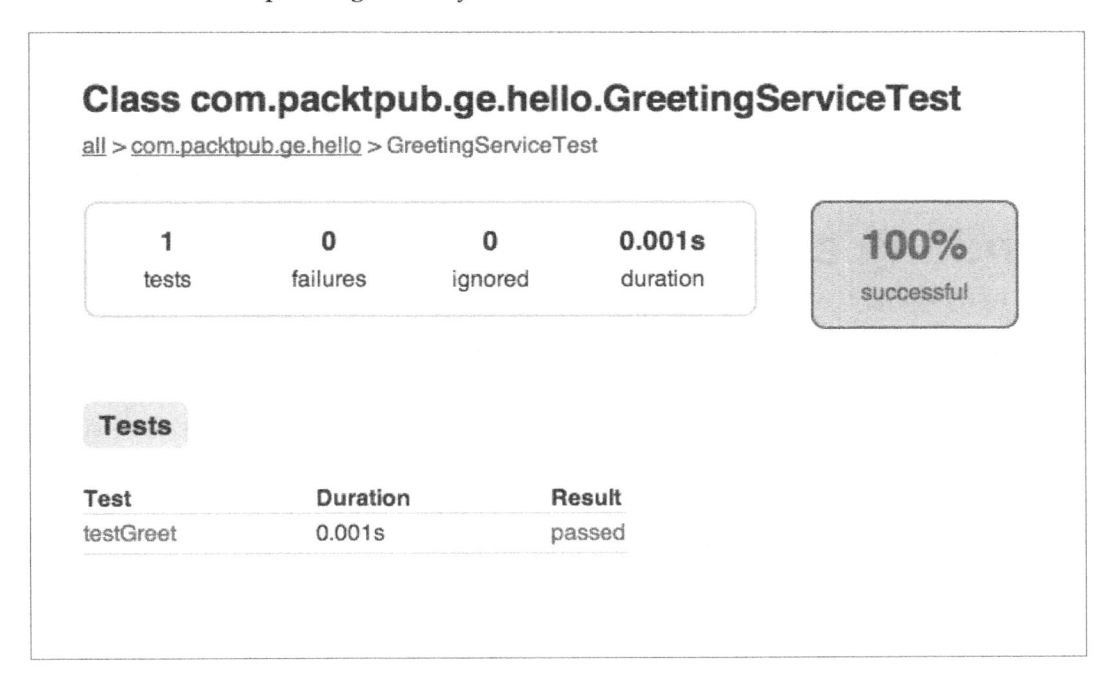

Class com.packtpub.ge.hello.GreetingServiceTest

all > com.packtpub.ge.hello > GreetingServiceTest

1	0	0	0.001s
tests	failures	ignored	duration

100% successful

Tests

Test	Duration	Result
testGreet	0.001s	passed

And the **Test Summary** will look something like this:

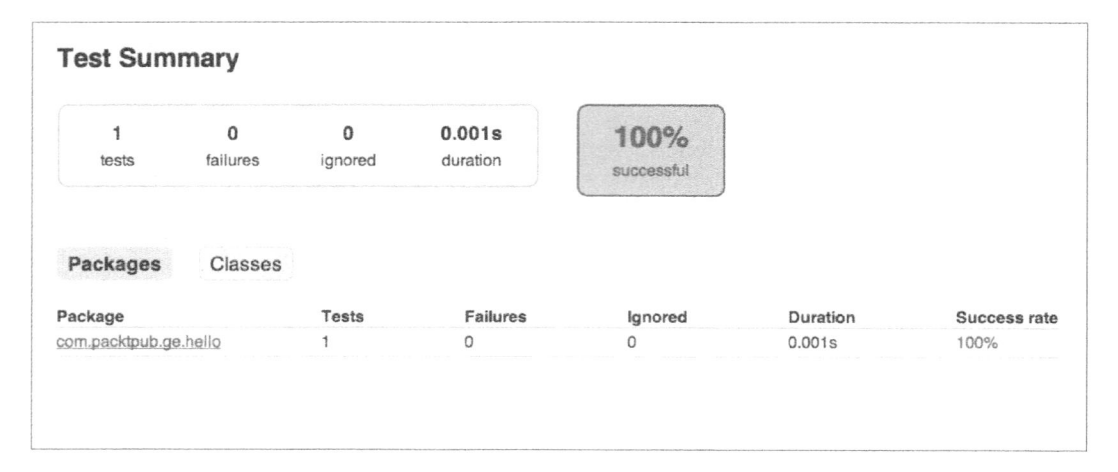

Test Summary				
1 tests	0 failures	0 ignored	0.001s duration	100% successful

Packages Classes

Package	Tests	Failures	Ignored	Duration	Success rate
com.packtpub.ge.hello	1	0	0	0.001s	100%

Bundling an application distributable

In the first example, we ran our application by using the `java` command directly from the command line. Usually, such command-line applications are shipped with scripts to run the application so that the end user need not always write the whole command by hand. Also, while developing, we repeatedly need to run the app. It would be nicer if we could write a task in our build file such that an app can be run in one Gradle invocation.

The good news is that there already exists such a plugin called `application`, shipped with Gradle, which can do both for us. For this example, we will copy over the `hello-test` project as `hello-app`. Let's make simple modifications to our `build.gradle` as follows:

```
apply plugin: 'java'
apply plugin: 'application'

mainClassName = "com.packtpub.ge.hello.Main"
run.args = ["Reader"]

repositories {
    mavenCentral()
}

dependencies {
    testCompile 'junit:junit:4.11'
}
```

The second line applies the `application` plugin to our build. To make this plugin work, we need to configure Gradle to use our `Main` entry point class, which has the static `main` method that needs to run when our application is run. We specified that on line #4 by setting the `mainClassName` property that is added to the build by the `application` plugin. Finally, when we want to run the app using Gradle (that is, while developing), we need to provide some command-line arguments to our app. The `application` plugin adds the `run` task to our build. As we said earlier, tasks are objects and they have properties and methods just like any regular object. On line #5, we set the `args` property of the `run` task to a list with one element `Reader`, so whenever we execute the run task, `Reader` will be passed as a command-line argument to our main method. Those who have used IDEs to set **Run Configuration** can easily relate to this. The rest of the file is the same as the last example.

> In the preceding example, as we are applying the `application` plugin, it is not necessary to explicitly apply the `java` plugin as an `application` plugin implicitly applies the `java` plugin to our build.
>
> It also implicitly applies the `distribution` plugin so that we get the tasks to package the application as a ZIP or TAR archive and also gets the task to install the application distribution locally.
>
> More information on the `application` plugin can be found at https://docs.gradle.org/current/userguide/distribution_plugin.html.

Now, if we check the tasks that are available in our build, we see a few additions under the `Application tasks` and `Distribution tasks` groups:

```
$ gradle tasks
...
Application tasks
-----------------
installApp - Installs the project as a JVM application along with libs
and OS specific scripts.
run - Runs this project as a JVM application
...


Distribution tasks
```

```
------------------
assembleDist - Assembles the main distributions
distTar - Bundles the project as a distribution.
distZip - Bundles the project as a distribution.
installDist - Installs the project as a distribution as-is.
...
```

Running the application with Gradle

Let's first look at the `run` task. We will call this task with the `-q` flag to suppress other messages by Gradle:

```
$ gradle -q run
Hello Reader
```

As expected, we see the output on a console. This task really shines when we make changes and can run our app in one command as follows:

```
public String greet(String user) {
    return "Hola " + user;
}
```

We changed our `GreetingService` for a moment to return "Hola" instead of "Hello" and see if run reflects the changes:

```
$ gradle -q run
Hola Reader
```

Yes, it did.

> One might wonder how to pass command-line arguments to run a task from the command line itself, instead of the build file, which is something as follows:
>
> **$ gradle -q run Reader**
>
> However, it doesn't work this way. As Gradle can accept multiple task names from a command line, there is no way for Gradle to know whether `Reader` was an argument that needs to be passed to run a task, or it's a task name itself. For example, the following command calls two tasks:
>
> **$ gradle -q clean build**
>
> There are, of course, some workarounds if you really need to pass the command line to the program at every invocation of a run task. One such way is to use the `-Pproperty=value` command-line option and then extract the property's value in the `run` task to send it as `args` to the program. The `-P` adds properties to the Gradle `Project`.
>
> To achieve this, update the `run.args` in `build.gradle` as follows:
>
>   run.args = [project.runArgs]
>
> Also, then from command line provide the property value by calling:
>
> **$ gradle -q run -PrunArgs=world**
>
> In the preceding example, we provided the value of a property at the time of calling the `gradle` command.
>
> Alternatively, we could create a `gradle.properties` in project's root parallel to the `build.gradle` file. In that case, for this example it would contain just `runArgs=world`. But it can declare more properties, which would be available in the build as properties on project object.
>
> There are other ways to declare properties as well, which can be found at https://docs.gradle.org/current/userguide/build_environment.html.

Building the distribution archive

Another interesting task is `distZip`, which packages the application along with OS-specific start scripts:

```
$ gradle distZip
:compileJava
:processResources UP-TO-DATE
:classes
:jar
```

```
:startScripts
:distZip

BUILD SUCCESSFUL

Total time: 1.29 secs
```

It would have generated the application distribution in ZIP format in the `build/distributions` relative to the project root. The name of the ZIP defaults to the project name. In this case, it would be `hello-app.zip`. This can be changed, if required, using the following property in `build.gradle`:

```
distributions.main.baseName = 'someName'
```

Let's unzip the archive to see its contents:

```
hello-app
├── bin
│   ├── hello-app
│   └── hello-app.bat
└── lib
    └── hello-app.jar
```

We see a pretty standard directory structure inside the ZIP. It contains a shell script and windows BAT script to run our app. Also, it contains the JAR file of our application. The `lib` directory also contains the application's runtime dependencies. We can configure the `distribution` plugin to add more files in our distributions such as Javadoc, README, and so on.

We can run the script to verify that it works. Using command prompt, we can execute this command in Windows. For that use the `cd` command, and change the directory to the `bin` directory of the extracted ZIP file.

```
$ hello-app Reader
Hello Reader
```

On Mac OS X/Linux, execute the following command:

```
$ ./hello-app Reader
Hello Reader
```

Generating IDE project files

IDEs are an integral part of a Java developer's tool chain and workflow. However, manually setting up an IDE to correctly identify the project structure and dependencies for any moderately sized project is not an easy task.

Checking-in IDE-specific files or directories such as `.classpath`, `.project`, `.ipr`, `.iws`, `.nbproject`, `.idea`, `.settings`, `.iml`, is not a good idea. We know that some still do it because it's hard to generate the IDE file manually every time someone checks the project out of the version control system. However, checking in such files creates problems as they eventually go out of sync from the main build file. Also, this forces the whole team to use the same IDE and manually update the IDE files whenever there is a change in the build.

How nice would it be if we could just check-in only those files that are necessary for a project to be built independent of IDE and let our build system generate a file specific to our favorite IDE? Our wish is granted. Also, here is the best part. The number of lines that you need to modify in your Gradle build file is only one. Gradle sports very nice plugins that can generate IDE-specific project files. Both IntelliJ IDEA and Eclipse are covered by their respective plugins. Depending on which IDE you want to support, you will either include `apply plugin: 'idea'` or `apply plugin: 'eclipse'`.

In fact, there is no harm in including both.

Now, from the command line, execute the following for Eclipse and IntelliJ IDEA, respectively:

```
$ gradle eclipse
```

```
$ gradle idea
```

It should generate IDE-specific files for you and now you can directly open a project in either of the IDEs.

> Make sure you ignore IDE-specific files in version control. For example, if you are using Git, consider adding the following entries in your `.gitignore` file to prevent someone from accidentally committing the IDE-specific files:
>
> ```
> .idea/
> *.iml
> *.ipr
> *.iws
> .classpath
> .project
> .settings/
> ```

Summary

We started off this chapter by building a very simple Java project. We saw how the intelligent conventions of the `java` plugin helped us keep the build file concise. Then, we added unit tests to this project and included the JUnit library from the Maven central repository. We made the tests fail and checked the reports to see the explanation. Then, we saw how the application's distribution can be created using the `application` plugin. Finally, we saw the `idea` and `eclipse` plugins that help us generate the IDE-specific files for our project.

Overall, we realized how powerful the plugin system in Gradle is. Gradle, out-of-the-box, ships with many interesting plugins, but we are not forced to use any of them. We will build a web application in the next chapter and also learn how configurations and dependency management works..

3
Building a Web Application

Now that we have seen the ease of using Gradle for building a command-line Java application, we shouldn't be surprised to know that building web applications based on Java servlet specification is also equally easy with Gradle.

In this chapter, we will build a simple web application first, which is distributed as a WAR file that can be deployed to any servlet container. Then, we will take a look at how dependencies and repositories are configured in a build file.

Building a simple Java web project

Again, we will keep our application as minimal as possible and create a web-enabled version of the application, which we developed in the last chapter. The application will provide the user a form to input their name and a **Submit** button. When the user clicks on the **Submit** button, the greeting will be displayed.

The application will be based on Servlet 3.1 specification. We will reuse the GreetService that we developed in the previous chapter. The form will be served by a static HTML file, which can post data to our servlet. The servlet will create a greeting message and forward it to a JSP for rendering.

> For more details on Servlet specification 3.1, go to https://jcp.org/aboutJava/communityprocess/final/jsr340/index.html.

Creating source files

Let's create the root of the project as `hello-web`. The structure is similar to what we had seen for a simple Java application, with one addition, which is the web app root. The Web app root, by default, is located at `src/main/webapp`. Those who are familiar with Maven will immediately notice that it's the same path used by Maven as well.

The Web app root (`webapp`) contains all the public resources required to run a web application, which includes dynamic pages such as JSPs or the files required for other view template engines such as Thymeleaf, FreeMarker, Velocity, and so on; as well as static resources such as HTML, CSS, JavaScript, and image files; and other configuration files such as `web.xml` in the special directory called `WEB-INF`. The files stored in `WEB-INF` are not directly accessible to the client; hence, it is a perfect place to store protected files.

We will begin with creating the directory structure for what the final application should look like:

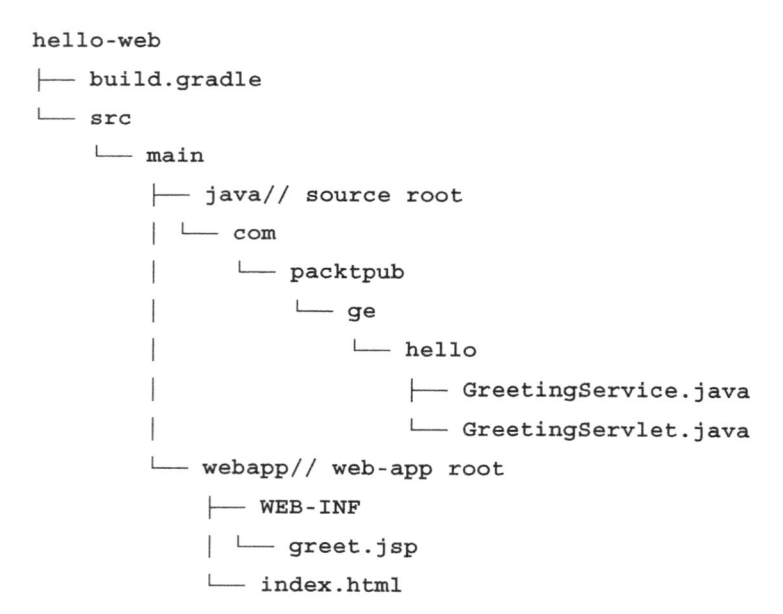

```
hello-web
├── build.gradle
└── src
    └── main
        ├── java// source root
        │   └── com
        │       └── packtpub
        │           └── ge
        │               └── hello
        │                   ├── GreetingService.java
        │                   └── GreetingServlet.java
        └── webapp// web-app root
            ├── WEB-INF
            │   └── greet.jsp
            └── index.html
```

Then, perform the following steps:

1. Let's first add the familiar `GreetingService` from the last chapter to our sources. We might notice that copying the Java source file is not a right way to reuse. There are much better ways to organize such dependencies. One such way is with multimodule projects. We will see this in *Chapter 5, Multiprojects Build*.

2. Now, add the following content to the `index.html` file:

   ```
   <!doctype html>
   <html>
     <head>
       <title>Hello Web</title>
     </head>
     <body>
       <form action="greet" method="post">
         <input type="text" name="name"/>
         <input type="submit"/>
       </form>
     </body>
   </html>
   ```

   This file starts with an HTML 5 `doctype` declaration, which is the most simple `doctype` we can use. Then, we create a form that will post to `greet` endpoint (it is a relative path to the page).

3. Now, at the heart of this application, there is the `GreetServlet` that responds to the post request:

   ```
   package com.packtpub.ge.hello;

   import javax.servlet.*;
   import javax.servlet.annotation.WebServlet;
   import javax.servlet.http.*;
   import java.io.IOException;

   @WebServlet("/greet")
   public class GreetingServlet extends HttpServlet {

     GreetingService service = new GreetingService();

     @Override
   ```

```
    public void doPost(HttpServletRequest request,
                    HttpServletResponse response)
      throws ServletException, IOException {

      String name = request.getParameter("name");
      String message = service.greet(name);
      request.setAttribute("message", message);

      RequestDispatcher dispatcher = getServletContext()
        .getRequestDispatcher("/WEB-INF/greet.jsp");

      dispatcher.forward(request, response);
    }

}
```

In the preceding code , the `WebServlet` annotation's value maps this servlet to the `/greet` path relative to the context of the application. Then, an instance of `GreetService` is made available in this servlet. The overridden method `doPost` extracts the name from the `request` object, generates the greeting message, sets this message back in the `request` as an attribute so that it's accessible in the JSP, and then finally forwards the request to the `greet.jsp` file that is located at `/WEB-INF/greet.jsp`.

4. This brings us to the `greet.jsp` file, which is kept in `WEB-INF` so that it's not directly accessible and the request has to always come through the servlet that sets the right request attributes:

```
<!doctype html>
<html>
  <head>
    <title>Hello Web</title>
  </head>
  <body>
    <h1>${requestScope.message}</h1>
  </body>
</html>
```

This JSP just prints the `message` that is available in the request attribute.

Creating a build file

Finally, let's create the file we've been waiting for—the `build.gradle` file—in the root of the project:

```
apply plugin: 'war'

repositories {
    mavenCentral()
}

dependencies {
    providedCompile 'javax.servlet:javax.servlet-api:3.1.0'
}
```

Let's try to understand this file now:

- The first line applies the `war` plugin to the project. This plugin adds a `war` task to the project. One might wonder why we don't need to apply the `java` plugin to compile the classes. This is because the `war` plugin extends the `java` plugin; so all the tasks that were available when we applied the `java` plugin are still available to us in addition to the `war` task.
- Next, comes the `repositories` section that configures our build to look for all the dependencies in the Maven central repository.

Lastly, in the `dependencies` block, we add `servlet-api` to the `providedCompile` configuration (scope). This tells Gradle not to package the servlet API with the application, as it will already be available on the container where the application will be deployed. The `providedCompile` configuration is added by the `war` plugin (it also adds `providedRuntime`). If we had any other dependency that needs to be packaged with our application, it would have been declared using the compile configuration. For example, if our app depends on the Spring Framework, then the dependencies section might have looked as follows:

```
dependencies {
    compile 'org.springframework:spring-context:4.0.6.RELEASE'
    providedCompile 'javax.servlet:javax.servlet-api:3.1.0'
}
```

Don't worry if it feels like the details on `repositories`, `configurations` and `dependencies` are a bit sketchy. We will soon see them again, in more detail, later in this chapter.

Building the artifact

Now that our source files are ready with the build file, we must build the deployable WAR file. Let's verify the tasks available for our build using the following command:

```
$ gradle tasks --all
```

...

```
war - Generates a war archive with all the compiled classes, the web-app content and the libraries. [classes]
```

...

We will notice the `war` task there, which depends on `classes` (task). We don't need to explicitly compile and build the Java sources, which is automatically taken care of by the `classes` task. So all that we need to do now is, use the following command:

```
$ gradle war
```

Once the build is complete, we will see the directory's structure similar to following structure:

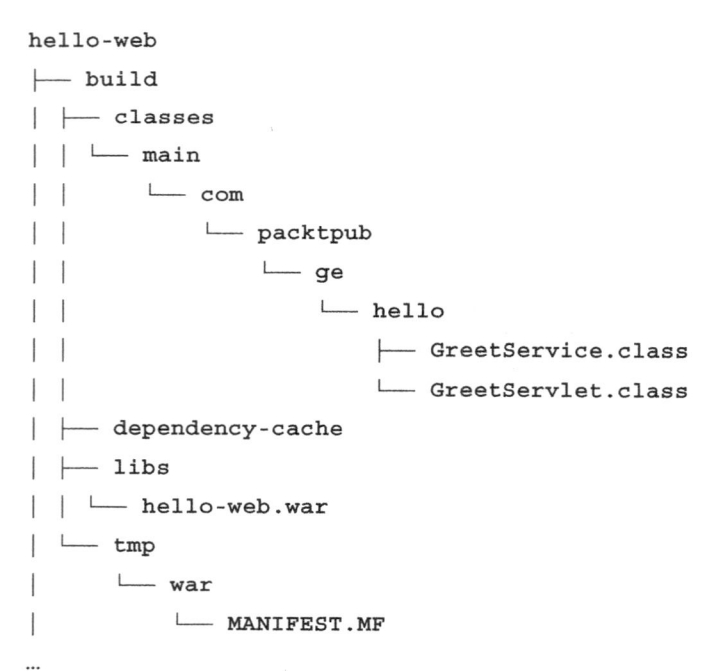

```
hello-web
├── build
│   ├── classes
│   │   └── main
│   │       └── com
│   │           └── packtpub
│   │               └── ge
│   │                   └── hello
│   │                       ├── GreetService.class
│   │                       └── GreetServlet.class
│   ├── dependency-cache
│   ├── libs
│   │   └── hello-web.war
│   └── tmp
│       └── war
│           └── MANIFEST.MF
...
```

The war file is created at `/build/libs/hello-web.war`.

> A `war` file is nothing but a ZIP file with a different file extension. The same holds true for an `.ear` or `.jar` file for that matter. We can use the standard zip/unzip tools too or use the JDK's `jar` utility to perform various operations on these files. To list the contents of WAR, use `jar -tf build/libs/hello-web.war`.

Let's check the content of this WAR file once:

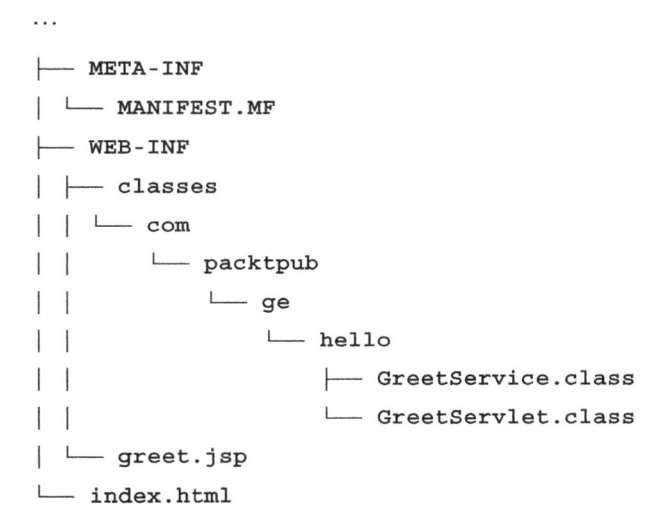

```
...
├── META-INF
│   └── MANIFEST.MF
├── WEB-INF
│   ├── classes
│   │   └── com
│   │       └── packtpub
│   │           └── ge
│   │               └── hello
│   │                   ├── GreetService.class
│   │                   └── GreetServlet.class
│   └── greet.jsp
└── index.html
```

Perfect. The compiled classes landed into the `WEB-INF/classes` directory. The servlet API's JAR is not included as it was in the `providedCompile` scope.

> **Exercise**
>
> Add `compile 'org.springframework:spring-context:4.0.6.RELEASE'` in the dependencies section and then do a `gradle war` file and see the content of the created WAR.

[43]

Running the web application

We have come a long way in creating the web-app. However, to use it, it must be deployed to a servlet container. It can be classically deployed to a servlet container by copying the `.war` file in the servlet container's designated directory (such as `webapps` in the case of Tomcat). Alternatively, a more recent technique can be used to embed a Servlet container into a Java app, which is packaged as a `.jar` and is run as any other `java -jar` command.

Web apps are typically run in three modes, development, functional testing, and production. The key characteristics of all the three modes differ as follows:

- The key characteristics of running web in development mode is faster deployment (preferably hot reloads), quick server start and shutdown, very low server footprint, and so on.

- While in functional testing, we typically deploy `web-app` once for the entire test suite's run. We need to mimic production-like behavior of an app as much as possible. We need to set up and destroy the web-app's state (such as databases), using lightweight databases (preferably in-memory) for all tests. We also need to mock external services.

- Whereas, in production deployments, the app-servers' (whether standalone or embedded) configuration, security, optimization of app, caches, and so on, takes more precedence, features such as hot reloading deployments are rarely used; faster startup time takes lesser precedence.

We will only cover the development scenario in this chapter. We will start with the traditional way to highlight its problems and then move on to Gradle's way.

Now, if we need to deploy the war in a manual way. We can choose any Java servlet container such as Jetty or Tomcat to run our web-app. In this example, let's use Tomcat. Assuming Tomcat is installed at `~/tomcat` or `C:\tomcat` (based on the OS that we are using):

1. If the server is running, ideally we should stop it.
2. Copy the WAR file to the Tomcat's `webapp` (`~/tomcat/webapps`) directory.
3. Then, start the Tomcat server using `~/tomcat/bin/startup.sh` or `C:\tomcat\bin\startup.bat`.

However, this kind of deployment feels outdated in Gradle's age. Especially, while developing the web-app, we have to constantly package the application as a war, copy the latest version to the container, and restart the container to get the latest code running. When we say build automation, it implicitly means that no manual intervention should be expected and things should work in one click (or one command in Gradle's case). Also, luckily, there are many options to achieve this level of automation.

Plugins to the rescue

Out of the box, Gradle has no support for modern servlet containers. However, this is the beauty of Gradle's architecture. Innovation and/or implementation does not have to come from a selected few who are creating Gradle. With the help of plugins API, anyone can create functionally rich plugins. We are going to use a plugin called Gretty for our web-app's development time deployment, but you should also check out others to see what works the best for you.

> There is a jetty plugin available, which is shipped with Gradle. However, it has not been actively updated; hence, it officially supports only Jetty 6.x (as of this writing). So we can use it if our web application is based on Servlet 2.5 specification or lower.

A Gretty plugin can be found at a Gradle plugin portal (look at the references below). This plugin adds numerous tasks to the build and supports various versions of Tomcat and Jetty. Installing it cannot be any easier. The code for this uses the same hello-web source from the last section, but updates the build.gradle file. An entire source code for this example can be found in the chapter-03/hello-gretty directory of the book's sample code.

Just include the following at the first line of build.gradle:

```
plugins {
   id "org.akhikhl.gretty" version "1.2.4"
}
```

Building a Web Application

That's it—we are done. This is relatively a new syntax for applying plugins to builds, which was added in Gradle 2.1. This is especially useful for applying third-party plugins. Unlike calling the `apply` method to apply the plugin, we start with the plugin block on the first line. Then, we specify the plugin's ID. For applying an external plugin, we must use the fully qualified plugin ID and version. We can include the `war` plugin's application inside this block. For internal plugins, we don't need to specify a version. It will look as follows:

```
plugins {
   id "org.akhikhl.gretty" version "1.2.4"
   id "war"
}
```

If we run `gradle tasks` now, we must have an `appRun` task under the `Gretty` group. There are many more tasks in this group, which are added by the Gretty plugin. If we run the `appRun` task, without configuring the plugin explicitly, then by default a Jetty 9 will be run on `http://localhot:8080`. We can open the browser and verify.

There are many configurations exposed by the plugin, in order to control aspects such as server version, port number, and many more. Add a `gretty` block to the `build.gradle` files as follows:

- If we want to use Tomcat 8 on port 8080, we'll add the following lines of code:

```
gretty {
   servletContainer = 'tomcat8'
   port = 8080
}
```

- If we want to use Jetty 9 on 9080, we'll add the following lines of code:

```
gretty {
   servletContainer = 'jetty9'
   port = 9080
}
```

There are many more configuration options available in Gretty; we would recommend you to check Gretty's online documentation. See the link to Gretty in the references section.

Here is how the running application looks like:

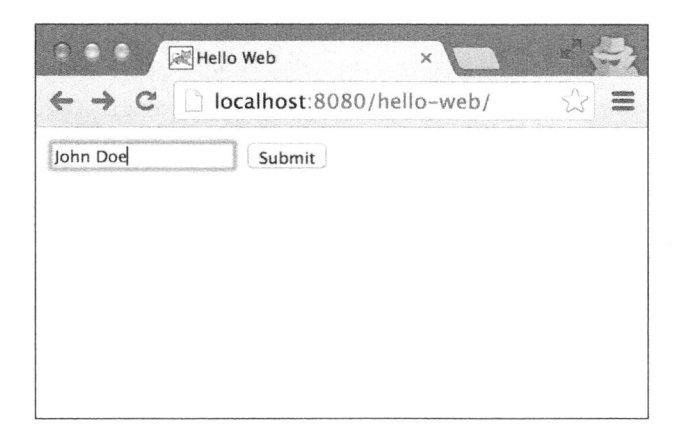

Once the **Submit** button is pressed, we'll get the following result:

References

For Gradle, refer to the following URL:

- Gradle plugin portal: `https://plugins.gradle.org/`

For Gretty, refer to the following URL:

- Gretty plugin: `https://plugins.gradle.org/plugin/org.akhikhl.gretty`
- Gretty documentation: `http://akhikhl.github.io/gretty-doc/`

There are various plugins available to automate the deployment. Some of them are listed here:

- Cargo plugin: `https://github.com/bmuschko/gradle-cargo-plugin`
- Arquillian plugin: `https://github.com/arquillian/arquillian-gradle-plugin`
- Tomcat plugin: `https://github.com/bmuschko/gradle-tomcat-plugin`

Project dependencies

In real life, we work on a lot more complex applications than what we have just seen. Such applications rely on other specialized components to provide some functionality. For example, an Enterprise Java application's build may depend on various components such as open source libraries in Maven central, libraries developed and hosted in-house, and (maybe) even on another subprojects. Such dependencies are, themselves, located at various locations like, local intranet, local filesystem, and so on. They need to be resolved, downloaded, and brought into the appropriate configuration (such as `compile`, `testCompile`, and so on) of the build.

Gradle does an excellent job in locating and making dependencies available in the appropriate `classpath` and packaging if required. Let's begin with the most common kind of dependencies—external libraries.

External libraries

Almost all real-world projects depend on external libraries for reusing the proven and tested components. Such dependencies include language utilities, database drivers, web frameworks, XML/JSON serialization libraries, ORMs, logging utilities, and many more.

The dependencies of a project are declared in the `dependencies` section in the build file.

Gradle provides an extremely succinct syntax for declaring the coordinates of an artifact. It usually takes a form of `group:name:version`. Note that each value is separated by a colon (`:`).

For example, Spring Framework's core library can be referenced using the following code:

```
dependencies {
  compile 'org.springframework:spring-core:4.0.6.RELEASE'
}
```

> For those who don't enjoy terseness, dependencies can be referred in a more descriptive format (called map format).
> ```
> compile group:'org.springframework', name:'spring-core', version:'4.0.6.RELEASE'
> ```

We can also specify multiple dependencies as follows:

```
configurationName dep1, dep2, dep3....
```

Where `configurationName` represents the configuration such as `compile`, `testCompile` and so on, we are soon going to see what configuration is in this context.

The dynamic version

The version of our dependencies keep on updating every now and then. Also, when we are in the development phase, we don't want keep on checking manually whether a new version is available.

In such situations, we can add a + to denote the version mentioned above, given the number of artifacts. For example, `org.slf4j:slf4j-nop:1.7+` declares any version of SLF4J that is above 1.7. Let's include this in a `build.gradle` file and check what Gradle brings in for us.

We run the following code in our `build.gradle` file:

```
runtime 'org.slf4j:slf4j-nop:1.7+'
```

Then, we run the `dependencies` task:

```
$ gradle dependencies
...
+--- org.slf4j:slf4j-nop:1.7+ -> 1.7.7
|    \--- org.slf4j:slf4j-api:1.7.7
...
```

We see that Gradle chose the 1.7.7 version, as it's the latest version available as of the writing of this book. If you observe the second line, it tells us that `slf4j-nop` depends on `slf4j-api`; hence, it's a transitive dependency for our project.

A word of caution here is, always use + for only minor version upgrades (such as `1.7+` in the preceding example). Letting the major version automatically update (for example, just image is spring automatically updates from 3 to 4, `compile 'org.springframework:spring-core:+'`) is nothing but a gamble. A dynamic dependency resolution is a nice feature, but it should be used with care. It should ideally only be used at the development stage of the project and not for releases candidates.

We get a flaky build whenever the dependency's version updates to some incompatible version with our app. We should target for reproducible builds, such a build should produce the exact same artifact, be it today or one year down the line.

Transitive dependencies

By default, Gradle resolves transitive dependencies quite intelligently, giving preference to the latest conflicting versions, if any. However, for some reason, if we want to disable transitive dependencies, all we need to provide is an extra block to our dependency declaration:

```
runtime ('org.slf4j:slf4j-nop:1.7+') {
    transitive = false
}
```

Now, if we check the output of the `dependencies` task, we see that no other dependency is included anymore:

`\--- org.slf4j:slf4j-nop:1.7.2`

We can also force a given version of the library so that, even if the same artifacts, the later version comes through the transitive dependency; the version we forced will win:

```
runtime ('org.slf4j:slf4j-nop:1.7.2') {
    force = true
}
```

Running dependencies task now will produce:

`+--- org.slf4j:slf4j-api:1.7.2`
`\--- org.slf4j:slf4j-nop:1.7.7`
`     \--- org.slf4j:slf4j-api:1.7.7 -> 1.7.2`

This shows the older version of `slf4j-api` won, even though a later version could have been fetched by the transitive dependency.

Dependency configurations

Gradle provides a very elegant way to declare dependencies that are required for building different groups of sources in various stages of a project build.

> These groups of sources are known as **source sets**. The simplest and well-understood examples of source sets are main and test. The main source set contains files that will be compiled and built as a JAR file and will be deployed somewhere or published to some repository. The test source set, on the other hand, contains files that will be executed by a testing tool such as JUnit, but will not make it to production. Now, both the source sets have different requirements for the dependencies, building, packaging, and execution. We will see how to add new source sets in *Chapter 7, Testing and Reporting with Gradle*, for integration testing.

As we have defined the group of related sources in a source set, dependencies are also defined as a group called **configuration**. Each configuration has its name such as compile, testCompile, and so on. Dependencies included in various configurations also differ. Configurations are grouped by the characteristics of dependencies. For example, the following are configurations that are added by the java and war plugins:

- compile: This is added by the java plugin. Adding a dependency to this configuration implies that the dependency is required to compile the source. In the case of war, these will also get copied in WEB-INF/lib. Examples of such dependencies are libraries such as Spring Framework, Hibernate, and so on.

- runtime: This is added by the java plugin. This includes the compile dependencies by default. Dependencies in this group are required at runtime for the compiled source code, but they are not required to compile it. Dependencies such as JDBC drivers are runtime dependencies only. We do not need them on our classpath to compile the source code as we code against the standard JDBC API interfaces available in JDK. However, for our application to run properly, we need a specific driver implementation at run time. For example, runtime 'mysql:mysql-connector-java:5.1.37' includes the MySQL driver.

- `testCompile`: This is added by the `java` plugin. This includes the `compile` dependencies by default. Dependencies added to this configuration are only available to test sources. Examples are testing libraries such as JUnit, TestNG, and so on, or any libraries that are exclusively used by test source such as Mockito. They are neither required to compile, nor required at runtime for the main source set. They do not get included in `war` in the case of building a `web-app`.
- `testRuntime`: This is added by the `java` plugin. This includes `testCompile` and `runtime` dependencies by default. Dependencies in this configuration are only required to test sources at the runtime (that is, while running tests). Hence, they are not included in the compilation classpath of tests. This is just like the runtime configuration, but only for test sources.
- `providedCompile`: This is added by the `war` plugin. Dependencies such as servlet APIs are provided by application servers and hence need not be packaged in our `war`. Anything that we expect to be already included in the server runtime can be added to this configuration. However, it has to be present at the time of compilation of the source code. Hence, we can declare such dependencies as `providedCompile`. Examples are servlet API and any Java EE implementations that are available at server runtime. Such dependencies are not included in `war`.
- `providedRuntime`: This is added by the `war` plugin. Dependencies that will be made available at application runtime by the server and application do not need to be included while compiling because there is no direct reference to the implementation. Such libraries can be added to this configuration. Such dependencies will not be included in `war`. Hence, we should make sure to have implementation available in the application runtime.

As we know, when we apply the `war` plugin, the `java` plugin also gets applied. That's why all six configurations are available when we are building a web application. More configurations can be added by plugins, or we can declare them ourselves in our build script.

Interestingly, configuration does not just include dependencies, but also the artifacts produced by this configuration.

Repositories

The repositories section configures the repositories where Gradle will look for dependencies. Gradle downloads the dependencies into its own cache so that the download doesn't need to happen every time Gradle is run. We can configure multiple repositories as follows:

```
repositories {
  mavenCentral()   // shortcut to maven central
  mavenLocal()     // shortcut to maven local (typically ~/.m2)
  jcenter()        // shortcut to jcenter
  maven {
    url "http://repo.company.com/maven"
  }
  ivy {
    url "http://repo.company.com/ivy"
  }
  flatDir {        // jars kept on local file system
    dirs 'libDir'
  }
}
```

Repositories such as Maven, Ivy, and flat directory (filesystem) are supported for dependency resolution and uploading artifacts. There are some more specific convenience methods available for commonly used Maven repositories such as `mavenCentral()`, `jcenter()`, and `mavenLocal()`. However, more Maven repos can be easily configured using the following syntax:

```
maven {
  url"http://intranet.example.com/repo"
}
```

Before the central repositories, projects used to manage the libraries on filesystem, which were mostly checked in along with the source code. Some projects still do it; although we discourage this, people have their reasons to do so and Gradle has no reason to not support that.

It is important to remember that Gradle does not automatically assume any repository to search and download dependencies from. We have to explicitly configure at least one repository in the `repositories` block where Gradle will search for artifacts.

> **Exercise**
> Include Apache Commons Lang library to convert the message to title case using the following method:
> ```
> WordUtils.capitalize(String str)
> ```
> Capitalize all the whitespace-separated words in a string.

Summary

In this chapter, we first developed a web application using Gradle. We generated the WAR artifact by building the application and then deployed it to a local Tomcat. Then, we learned a few basics about dependency management, configurations, and supported repositories in Gradle.

> The reader should spend some more time reading these concepts in detail at Gradle's official documentation at `https://docs.gradle.org/current/userguide/userguide`.

For now, we should be good to build the most common type of Java applications with Gradle. In the next chapter, we will try to understand the Groovy DSL that Gradle provides and also understand the basic project model.

4
Demystifying Build Scripts

In the first three chapters, we saw many interesting functionalities that Gradle can add to our builds merely by adding a few lines in the build file. However, this was just the tip of the iceberg. What we explored was mostly the tasks that were added by plugins shipped with Gradle. From our experiences, we know that project builds are never this simple. They will have customizations no matter how hard we try to avoid them. That's why the ability to add custom logic is extremely important for a build tool.

Also, the beauty of Gradle lies exactly there. It doesn't come into our way whenever we decide to either extend the existing functionality or deviate completely from the convention and want to do something unconventional. We are not required to write the XML soup or the bunch of Java code if we wish to add some logic to our build. We can create our own tasks or extend the existing tasks to do more.

This flexibility comes with a very gentle learning curve in the form of learning Groovy DSL. In this chapter, we are going to understand the syntax of the Gradle build scripts and some of the key concepts of Gradle. We will cover the following topics:

- A Groovy primer that will help us understand the Gradle build script syntax
- The two important objects available in our build, namely, the `project` object and the `task` object(s)
- Build phases and life cycle callbacks
- Some details of the tasks (tasks execution and task dependencies)

Groovy for Gradle build scripts

To be proficient with Gradle and write effective build scripts, we need to understand some basics of Groovy, which is a fantastic dynamic language in itself. If we have any experience with dynamic languages such as Ruby or Python, in addition to Java, we will feel right at home with Groovy. If not, still knowing that most of the Java syntax is also the valid Groovy syntax should make us feel happy about Groovy, because we can start writing Groovy code and be productive from day one without having to learn anything.

To an unprepared eye, Gradle scripts may look a little difficult to comprehend at first. Gradle build scripts do not merely use the Groovy syntax, but also use a rich and expressive DSL that provides high-level abstractions to represent common build-related logics. Let's take a quick look at what makes Groovy a great choice for writing build files.

> Using Groovy for writing build logics is not new. Gant and GMaven have already used Groovy to write the build logic in order to harness Groovy's syntactic terseness and expressiveness. GMavenPlus is a successor of GMaven. The tools they are built upon, namely Ant and Maven, limit both Gant and GMaven respectively.
>
> Instead of piggybacking on the existing tools to just add syntactic enhancements, Gradle is designed by leveraging the learning from the past tools.

Why Groovy?

Gradle's core is written mostly in Java (see the information below). Java is a great language, but it is not the best fit for writing scripts. Just imagine scripting in Java, we would perhaps be writing another project for defining the build of our main project because of the verbosity and ceremony of Java. XML, which was heavily used in the previous generation of build tools (Ant and Maven), is okay for the declarative part but is not great for writing logic.

> We can view and download Gradle's source code from GitHub at https://github.com/gradle/gradle.

Groovy is a dynamic avatar of Java. As mentioned earlier, most of the Java syntax is the valid Groovy syntax too. If we know Java, we can already write Groovy code. This is a big plus provided that the sheer number of people who can write Java today.

Groovy's syntax is concise, expressive, and powerful. Groovy is a great mix of dynamic flavor, while still being able to use types. It is one of few languages that sport optional typing, that is, the flexibility to provide type information if we want to and leave type information aside when we don't want to. Groovy is an excellent language to build internal DSLs into because of the first class lambda support and metaprogramming capabilities. All of the above factors make it one of the most suitable candidates for writing build scripts.

Groovy primer

Although we can write Java style code in Groovy, if we invest some time in learning the dynamic nature of the language and some of the syntactical enhancements that Groovy offers, we will be able to write better Gradle build scripts and plugins. This is going to be fun if we don't already know Groovy.

Let's learn just enough of Groovy so that we can understand the Gradle scripts properly. We will take a quick look at a few language features of Groovy.

It is highly recommended to try and execute the code in the subsections that follow. Also, writing and trying out more code on our own to explore Groovy would help us strengthen our understanding of the language fundamentals. This guide is not exhaustive by any means and is included just to set the Groovy ball rolling.

Running Groovy code

The easiest and recommended way is to install the latest Groovy SDK locally. Groovy code snippets can be executed using any of the following options:

- Save the snippets to the .groovy script and run from the command line using the following code:

    groovy scriptname.groovy

- We can use the Groovy console GUI that comes packaged with the Groovy installation to edit and run the scripts
- We can also use Groovy shell, which is an interactive shell for executing or evaluating Groovy statements and expressions

If we don't want to install Groovy locally, then:

- We can run Groovy code online in a browser using Groovy console at http://groovyconsole.appspot.com
- We can also run Groovy code in the build script by creating tasks and putting code snippets in them (we can also put them outside any task and it will still run it in the configuration phase)

Variables

In a Groovy script, the `def` keyword can define a variable (depending on the context):

```
def a = 10
```

However, the type of `a` is decided at the runtime depending on what type of object it points to. Roughly speaking, a reference declared as `def` can refer to any `Object` or its subclasses.

Declaring a more specific type is equally valid and should be used whenever we want to have type safety:

```
Integer b = 10
```

We can also use Java primitive data types, but keep in mind that they are not actually primitives in Groovy. They are still first-class objects and are actually Java wrapper classes for corresponding data type. Let's confirm with an example, as follows:

```
int c = 10
println c.getClass()
```

It prints the following output:

```
class java.lang.Integer
```

This shows that `c` is an object as we can call a method on it, and the type of `c` is `Integer`.

We recommend using specific types wherever possible as this adds to the readability and helps the Groovy compiler to detect errors early by catching invalid assignments. It also helps IDEs with code completion.

Strings

Unlike Java, the single quotes are (' ') string literals and not a `char`:

```
String s = 'hello'
```

Of course, regular Java string literals (" ") can also be used, but they are called GStrings in Groovy. They have an additional capability of string interpolation or inline expansion of variables or expressions:

```
def name = "Gradle"
println "$name is an awesome build tool"
```

This prints the following output:

Gradle is an awesome build tool

Both `${var}` and `$var` are valid, but wrapping (`${}`) is more suitable and required for complex or longer expressions. For example:

```
def number = 4
println "number is even ? ${number % 2 == 0 }"
```

It will print the following:

number is even ? true

All of us would remember adding + `"\\n"` at the end of every line in order to produce multiline strings in Java. Gone are those days, as Groovy supports multiline string literals. The multiline literal starts off with three single or double quotes (the same string versus the GString functionality) and ends with three single or double quotes:

```
def multilineString = '''\
    Hello
    World
'''
println multilineString
```

It will print the following:

Hello

World

The forward slash on line number 1 is optional and is used to exclude the first new line. If we do not put the forward slash, we would have an additional new line in the beginning of the output.

Also, look at the `stripMargin` and `stripIndent` methods for the special handling of leading whitespaces.

If our literal contains a lot of escape characters (for example, regex), then we are better off using a "slashy" string literal, which starts and ends with a single forward slash (/):

```
def r = /(\d)+/
println r.class
```

It will prints the following:

class java.lang.String

In the above example, if we had to use a regular string, then we would have to escape the backslash before the character class d. It would have looked as follows:

```
"(\\d)+"
```

Regular expressions

Groovy supports a pattern operator (~), which when applied to a string, gives a pattern object:

```
def pattern = ~/(\d)+/
println pattern.class
```

It prints the following:

```
class java.util.regex.Pattern
```

We can also use the find operator to directly match a string to a pattern:

```
if ("groovy" ==~ /gr(.*)/)
    println "regex support rocks"
```

It will print the following:

```
regex support rocks
```

Closures

Closure in Groovy is a block of code that can be assigned to a reference or passed around just like any other variable. The concept is known as **lambda** in many other languages, including Java 8 or function pointers.

> Lambdas have been supported since Java 8, but the syntax is a bit different than that of Groovy's closures. You don't need to be on Java 8 to use closure in Groovy.

If we have no exposure to any of the above, then some detailed reading will be required to understand the concept well because it lays the foundation for many other advanced topics going forward. Closure is a huge topic in itself and an in-depth discussion is beyond the scope of this book.

Closure is almost like a regular method or function, but it can also be assigned to a variable. Also, as it can be assigned to a variable, it must be an object as well; hence, it will have methods on itself:

```
def cl1 = {
    println "hello world!"
}
```

Here, the code block is being assigned to a variable called `cl1`. Now the code block can be executed using the call method in the future or the `cl1` variable can be passed around and executed later:

```
cl1.call()
```

No wonder it prints the following:

```
hello world!
```

As closures are like methods, they can also accept parameters:

```
def cl2 = { n ->
    println "value of param : $n"
}
cl2.call(101)
```

It prints the following:

```
value of param : 101
```

Just like methods, they can also return values. The last expression of closure is automatically returned if no explicit `return` statement is declared.

Closures start shining when we have methods that accept closures. For example, the `times` method is available on integer, which takes in a closure and executes it as many number times as the value of the integer itself; with every call, it passes the current value as if we were looping up to the value from `0`:

```
3.times(cl2)
```

It prints the following:

```
value of param : 0
value of param : 1
value of param : 2
```

We can also inline the block and pass it directly to a method:

```
3.times { println it * it }
```

It prints the following:

```
0
1
4
```

There is a special variable called `it`, which is available in the blocks scope if the closure doesn't define its parameter. In the preceding example, we accessed the number being passed to the block using `it` and multiplied it by itself to obtain its square.

Closures are extremely useful in situations such as callback handling, whereas in Java 7 and lower, we would have to use anonymous interface implementation to achieve the same result.

Data structures

Groovy supports literal declaration of the often-used data structures, which makes the code a lot more terse without sacrificing readability.

List

Groovy backs on the thoroughly tested Java Collection API and uses the same classes under the hood, but with some extra methods and syntactic sugar:

```
def aList = []
println aList.getClass()
```

It prints the following:

`class java.util.ArrayList`

> In Groovy, `[]` is actually a Java's `List` instance and not an array.

Let's create another list with some initial content:

```
def anotherList = ['a','b','c']
```

Thanks to operator overloading, we can use many of the operators intuitively on the list. For example, using `anotherList[1]` will give us b.

The following are some more examples of handy operators. This adds two lists and assigns the result to the list variable:

```
def list = [10, 20, 30] + [40, 50]
```

This appends 60 to the list:

```
list  <<  60
```

The following two examples simply subtracts a list from another list:

```
list = list - [20, 30, 40]
list  -= [20,30,40]
```

Iterating over a list is equally simple and intuitive:

```
list.each {println it}
```

It will print the following

10

50

60

The closure passed to `each` is executed for each element of the list, with the element as a parameter to closure. So, the preceding code iterates over the list and prints the value of each element. Notice the usage of `it`, which is a handle to the current element of the list.

Set

Defining a set is similar to that of a list, but in addition, we have to use `as Set`:

```
def aSet = [1,2,3] as Set
println aSet.class
```

This will print the following:

class java.util.LinkedHashSet

As the implementation class selected is `LinkedHashSet`, `aSet` will maintain the insertion order.

Alternatively, declare the type of variable to get the correct implementation:

```
TreeSet anotherSet = [1,2,3]
println anotherSet.class
```

This prints the following:

class java.util.TreeSet

Adding elements to a set is just like a list using an indirection operator. Other set interface methods are also available:

```
aSet << 4
aSet << 3
println aSet
```

This prints the following:

```
[1, 2, 3, 4]
```

We don't see the entry 4 twice as the collection is a set implementation, which by definition eliminates duplicates.

Map

Map is one of the most important data structures for any dynamic language. Hence, it gets a deserved place in Groovy's syntax. Map can be declared using the map literal `[:]`:

```
def a = [:]
```

The implementation chosen by default is `java.util.LinkedHashMap`, which preserves the insertion order:

```
def tool = [version:'2.8', name:'Gradle', platform:'all']
```

Note that the keys are not string literals, but they get automatically converted to a string:

```
println tool.name
println tool["version"]
println tool.get("platform")
```

We can access the values by using both the subscript and dot operator, in addition to the plain old `get()` method.

We can put and update data in map using the subscript and dot operator and, of course, the good old `put()`:

```
tool.version = "2.9"
tool["releaseDate"] = "2015-11-17"
tool.put("platform", "ALL")
```

Methods

The following is more of a Java-like method, which is of course a valid Groovy method:

```
int sum(int a, int b) {
  return a + b;
}
```

The preceding method can be succinctly rewritten as follows:

```
def sum(a, b) {
  a + b
}
```

Instead of specifying the return type, we just declared `def`, which effectively means the method can return any `Object` or subclass reference. Then, we omitted the type of the formal parameter, as declaring `def` is optional for formal parameters to a method. On line number 2, we omitted the `return` statement as the evaluation of the last expression is automatically returned by a method. We also omitted the semicolon as it's optional.

Both the examples are valid Groovy method declarations. However, readers are advised to choose types wisely as they provide type safety and act as a living documentation for methods. If we don't declare types of parameters, as in the preceding method, the sum (1,"2") will also become a valid method call, and worse, it returns an unexpected result without any exceptions.

Calling methods

A method call in Groovy can omit the parenthesis is many cases. Both of the following cases are valid method calls.

```
sum(1,2)
sum 1, 2
```

Default values of parameters

Many a time, we want to make a parameter optional by providing a default value so that if the caller does not provide the value, the default value will be used. Take a look at the following example:

```
def divide(number, by=2) {
    number/by
}

println divide (10, 5)
println divide (10)
```

It prints the following:

2
5

If we provide the value of the `by` parameter that will be used, the default value 2 will be assumed for the parameter.

Methods with map parameters/named parameters

Groovy does not support named parameters such as Python, but Map provides a very close approximation to the same functionality:

```
def method(Map options) {
    def a = options.a ?: 10
    def b = options.b ?: 20
}
```

In the preceding code, we expect the map to contain keys a and b.

> On line number 2 and 3, notice the elvis operator `?:`, which returns the left hand side value, if value exists and is *truthy*; otherwise returns the right hand side (default) value. It is basically short hand for the following code:
> ```
> options.a ? options.a : 10
> ```

Now, this method can be called as follows:

```
method([a:10,b:20])
```

We can omit the square brackets (`[]`) because maps have special support in the method call:

```
method(a:10, b:20)
```

Now, it clearly looks like the named parameters. The order of parameters is not important and all the parameters need not be passed. Also, the parenthesis wrapping is optional, just like any method call:

```
method b:30, a:40
method b:30
```

Methods with varags

Like in Java, varags are denoted by `...`, but providing the type is optional:

```
def sumSquares(...numbers) {
    numbers.collect{ it * it }.sum()
}
sumSquares 1, 2, 3
```

In the preceding examples, numbers are arrays, which have the `collect` method that accepts a closure and transforms each element of the collection in order to produce a new collection. In this case, we transform numbers in the collection of squares. Finally, we use the in-built sum method to sum all the squares.

Methods with closure params

Closures are important and, hence, Groovy has a special syntax for closures if the closure is the last parameter of a method signature:

```
def myMethod (param, cls) {
    ...
}
```

Then, this method can be called as follows:

```
myMethod(1,{ ... })
myMethod 2, {... }
myMethod(3) {...}
```

Out of these, the third one is the special syntactical support in which the parenthesis just wraps the other parameters, while the closure is written outside the parenthesis, as if it were a method body.

Classes

Classes in Groovy are declared just like Java classes, but with a lot lesser ceremony. Classes are public by default. They can inherit from other classes using `extends` or implementing interfaces using `implmenets`.

The following is the definition of a very simple class, `Person`, having two properties, `name` and `age`:

```
class Person {
   def name, age
}
```

Instead of using the `def` for properties, we can use more specific types.

Constructors

In addition to the default constructor, classes in Groovy get a special constructor, which takes the map of properties of the class. Here is how we use it:

```
def person = new Person(name:"John Doe", age:35)
```

In the preceding code, we have created the `person` object using the special constructor. The parameters are key-value pairs where the keys are the name of the properties in the class. The values provided for the keys will be set for the corresponding properties.

Properties

Groovy has language-level support for properties. In the preceding class, `name` and `age`, unlike Java, are not just fields, but are also properties of the class with their getters and setters in place. Fields are private by default and their public accessors and mutators (getters and setters) are generated automatically.

We can call the `getAge()`/`setAge()` and `getName()`/`setName()` methods on the `person` object that we created above. However, there is an even more succinct way to do so. We can access properties just as if they were public fields, but behind the scenes, Groovy routes it through the getters and setters. Let's try:

```
println person.age
person.age = 36
println person.age
```

It prints the following:

35

36

In the preceding code, on line number 1, `person.age` is actually a call to `person.getAge()` and, hence, it returns the age of the person. Then, we updated the age using `person.age` with an assignment operator and value on the right-hand side. We did not update the field, but it internally passes through the setter `setAge()`. This is only possible because groovy offers syntactical support for properties.

We can provide our own getters and/or setter for the desired fields, which will take precedence over the generated one, but it is only necessary if we have some logic to write in those. For example, if we want to have one positive value of age to be set, then we can provide our own `setAge()` implementation, and this will be used whenever the property is updated:

```
void setAge(age){
  if (age < 0)
    throw new IllegalArgumentException("age must be a positive number")
  else
    this.age = age
}
```

The support for properties results in the significant reduction of the boilerplate code from class definitions and enhances readability.

> Properties are first-class citizens in Groovy. Going forward, whenever we refer to property, do not get confused between properties and fields.

Instance methods

We can add an instance and static methods to classes just like we do in Java:

```
def speak(){
  println "${this.name} speaking"
}
static def now(){
  new Date().format("yyyy-MM-dd HH:mm:ss")
}
```

The methods section, as we discussed above, did not use classes, but applied as-is for the methods inside classes.

> **Scripts are classes**
> In fact, the methods that we discussed above were inside a class and they were not free-floating functions. As scripts get translated to classes transparently, it feels as if we were using functions.

I am sure you have enjoyed Groovy so far. There is a lot more to cover in Groovy, but we have to switch back our focus to Gradle. However, I hope to have generated enough curiosity about Groovy so that you can appreciate it as a language and explore more of it on your own. There are a few good resources included in the references section.

Another look at applying plugins

Now that we have learned about basic Groovy, let's put it to use in the context of the Gradle build script. In earlier chapters, we have already seen the syntax of applying a plugin. It looked something as follows:

```
apply plugin: 'java'
```

If we look carefully, `apply` is a method call. We can wrap the parameters in the parenthesis:

```
apply(plugin: 'java')
```

A method that takes in a map can pass key values just like named arguments. However, for a more clear representation of Map, we can wrap the parameters in `[]`:

```
apply([plugin: 'java'])
```

Finally, the `apply` method is implicitly applied on the `project` object (we will soon see this in the upcoming sections in this chapter). So, we can also call it on the `project` object's reference:

```
project.apply([plugin: 'java'])
```

So, from the preceding example, we can see that the statement that applies a plugin to project is merely a syntactic sugar to what is a method call on the `project` object. We are just writing Groovy code using Gradle API. Also, once we realize that, our perspective towards understanding the build script syntax changes for good.

Gradle – an object-oriented build tool

If we were to think of a build system in an object-oriented way, the following classes will immediately come to our minds:

- A `project` that represents a system that is being built
- A `task` that encapsulates pieces of build logics that need to be performed

Well, we are lucky. As we might expect, Gradle creates objects of both `project` and `task` types. These objects are accessible in our build script for us to customize. Of course, the underlying implementation is non-trivial and the API is very sophisticated.

A `project` object is a central piece of API that is exposed to and configured via the build scripts. A `project` object is available in the script such that the methods without object reference are intelligently invoked on the `project` object. We have just seen an example of this in the last section. Most of the build script syntax can be understood by just reading the project API.

The `task` objects are created for each task declared directly in the build file and also for plugins. We have already created a very simple task in *Chapter 1, Running Your First Gradle Task* and used tasks coming from plugins in *Chapter 2, Building Java Projects*, and *Chapter 3, Building a Web Application*.

> As we have seen, some tasks are already available in our build without us having to add a single line to our build file (such as the `help` task and the `tasks` task, and so on). Even for these tasks, we would have task objects.

We will soon see how and when these objects are created.

Build phases

A Gradle build follows a very simple life cycle on every invocation. The build passes through three stages: initialization, configuration, and execution. When a `gradle` command is invoked, not all the code written in our build file executes sequentially from top to bottom. Only the blocks of code that are relevant to the current phase of the build are executed. Also, the build phase's order determines when the block of code will execute. An example is the task configuration versus task execution. Understanding of these phases is important to correctly configure our build.

Initialization

Gradle first figures out whether the current project has child projects or if it is the only project in the build. For multiprojects build, Gradle figures out which projects (or sub-module, as many prefer to call them) have to be included in the build. We will see multiproject builds in the next chapter. Gradle then creates a `Project` instance for the root project and for each of the child projects of a project. For single module projects that we have seen so far, there is not much to configure in this phase.

Configuration

In this phase, the build scripts of participating projects are evaluated against the corresponding project object that was created during the initialization phase. In the case of multimodule projects, evaluation happens in breadth-wise fashion, that is, all the sibling projects will be evaluated and configured before child projects. However, this behavior is configurable.

Demystifying Build Scripts

Note that executing the scripts does not mean that the tasks are also executed. To quickly verify this, we can just put a `println` statement in the `build.gradle` file and also create a task that prints a message:

```
task myTask << {
  println "My task is executed"
}
// The following statement will execute before any task
println "build script is evaluated"
```

If we execute the following code:

`$ gradle -q myTask`

We would see the following output:

`build script is evaluated`

`My task is executed`

In fact, choose any in-built task as well, such as `help`:

`$ gradle -q help`

We would still see our `build script is evaluated` message before any task is executed. Why is that?

When a script is evaluated, all the statements in the script are executed sequentially. That's why the `println` statement at the root level gets executed. A task action, if you notice, is actually a closure; hence, it is only attached to a task during the statement execution. However, the closure itself is not executed yet. The statements inside the action closure executes only if the task is executed, which happens only in the next phase.

Tasks are only configured during this stage. No matter what tasks are going to be called, all tasks will be configured. Gradle prepares a **Directed Acyclic Graph (DAG)** representation of the tasks to determine the task dependency and execution order.

Execution

In this phase, Gradle figures out which tasks need to be run based on the parameters such as task names passed as command line arguments and the current directory. This is where tasks' actions will be performed. Hence, here, the action closures will actually execute if the task is to run.

> On subsequent invocations, Gradle intelligently determines which tasks need to actually run and which can be skipped. For example, for a compile task, there is no point in compiling again if there is no change in the source file after the last build. In such a case, the execution may be skipped. We can see such tasks in the output tagged as UP-TO-DATE:
>
> ```
> :compileJava UP-TO-DATE
> :processResources UP-TO-DATE
> :classes UP-TO-DATE
> :compileTestJava UP-TO-DATE
> :processTestResources UP-TO-DATE
> :testClasses UP-TO-DATE
> :test UP-TO-DATE
> ```
>
> In the preceding output, as there was no change from the previous build, Gradle actually skipped every task. However, this will not happen for a custom task that we write, unless we tell Gradle the logic for figuring out whether the task needs execution or not.

Life cycle callbacks

Gradle provides various hooks for executing code at various points during life cycle events. We can implement callback interfaces or provide callback closure to DSL in the build script. For example, we can listen for events such as the before and after project evaluation using the `beforeEvaluate` and `afterEvaluate` methods on `project`. We are not going to look at them individually, but the `Project` and `Gradle` (the interface name is not to be confused with the tool's name itself) APIs and the DSL documentation is the right place to check out the available callbacks, if we feel the need to implement life cycle callbacks.

Gradle Project API

As discussed earlier, Gradle creates a `project` object for each `build.gradle` for us during the initialization phase. This object is available in our build scripts using the `project` reference. Being a central piece of API, there are numerous methods and properties available on this object.

Project methods

We have been using the project API even without realizing that we are calling methods on the `project` object. Based on a few governing rules, all the top-level method calls in the build scripts are called on a project object if no explicit reference is provided.

Let's rewrite the very simple build file from *Chapter 1, Running Your First Gradle Task* to use the project reference for method calls:

```
project.apply plugin: 'java'

project.repositories {
    mavenCentral()
}

project.dependencies {
    testCompile 'junit:junit:4.11'
}
```

As we saw earlier in this chapter, `apply` is the method on the `project`. The so-called `dependencies` block is actually a method named `dependencies()` on `project` that accepts a closure. It is true for the `repositories` section as well. We can add parenthesis around the closure block to make it look like a plain old method call:

```
project.repositories({...})
project.dependencies({...})
```

There are many more interesting methods on this object, which we will see in the upcoming sections and chapters, again, with or without explicit reference to the `project` object.

Project properties

There are several properties available on the `project` object. Some properties are read-only properties, such as `name`, `path`, `parent`, and so on, while others are both readable and writable.

For example, we can set `project.description` to provide a description of our project. We can use the `project.version` property to set the version of the project. This version will be used by other tasks such as `Jar` to include a version number in the produced artifact.

> We cannot change the `project.name` from the `build.gradle` file, but we can use `settings.gradle` in the same project to set the project name. We will see this file in more detail when we learn about multi-project builds.

Apart from directly accessing a property by its name, we can access properties using the following methods on the `project` object.

To check whether a property exists, use the following method:

```
boolean hasProperty(String propertyName)
```

To get the value of a property for a given property name, use the following method:

```
Object property(String propertyName)
```

To set the value of a property for a given property name, use the following method:

```
void setProperty(String name, Object value)
```

For example, let's create a `build.gradle` file with the following content:

```
description = "a sample project"
version = "1.0"

task printProperties << {
    println project.version
    println project.property("description")
}
```

Execute the following task:

```
$ gradle -q printProperties
1.0
a sample project
```

As seen earlier, in Groovy, we can use the `property = value` syntax to call a setter. We are setting the `description` and `version` properties on the `project` object. Then, we add a task with the task action that prints the version using the `project` reference and `description` using the `property()` method on the `project` object.

The properties that we have seen above must exist on the project, otherwise build fails with a `Could not find property ...` message.

Extra properties on a project

Gradle makes it very easy to store user-defined properties on a project, while still being able to enjoy the niceties of project properties' syntax. All we have to do is to use the `ext` namespace to assign a value to a custom property. Then, this property can be accessed on a project just like regular project properties. Here is an example:

```
ext.abc = "123"
task printExtraProperties << {
    println project.abc
    println project.property("abc")
    println project.ext.abc
}
```

Execute the following task:

$ gradle -q printExtraProperties

123

123

123

In the preceding example, we declared a custom property called `abc` and assigned it the value `123`. We did not use the `project` reference as it is implicitly available at the script root level. In the task action, we printed it first using a project reference directly, just as if it were a property on `Project`. Then, we accessed using the `property()` method and also using the `project.ext` reference. Note that inside tasks' action closure, we should use the `project` reference to avoid any ambiguity.

Extra properties will be accessible in the sub-projects (modules). Extra properties can be set on other objects as well.

> We could have just used the local variable by declaring it with `def`. However, such variables are not accessible outside the lexical scope. Also, they are not queriable.

Although we have looked at a few methods and properties, it's impractical to cover all of those here; hence, it is worth spending some time reading the API and the DSL documentation of the `project` interface.

Tasks

As we have seen so far, a `task` is a named action that performs some build logic. It's a unit of build work. For example, `clean`, `compile`, `dist`, and so on, are typical build tasks that easily come to our mind if we have to write tasks for our project. Tasks are more or less analogous to Ant's targets.

The simplest way to create a task is as follows:

```
task someTask
```

Before we go any further with tasks, let's take a moment to ponder about task creation.

We used the `taskName` task form of a statement.

If we rewrite it as a `task (taskName)`, it will immediately look like the method call.

The preceding method, as we might have already guessed by now, is available on the project object.

So, we could write one of the following as well:

- `project.task "myTask"`
- `project.task("myTask")`

Notice that in the later examples we had to pass the task name as a string. The `task taskName` is a special form where we can use `taskName` as a literal instead of string. This is done by Groovy AST transformation magic.

The project has several flavors of a task method to create a task object:

```
Task task(String name)

Task task(String name, Closure configureClosure)

Task task(Map<String, ?> args, String name)

Task task(Map<String, ?> args, String name, Closure configureClosure)
```

However, in essence, we may pass some key values as named parameters while creating a task and a configuration closure to configure the task.

We are essentially creating an object of the type `Task` (the exact class name is not important right now). We can query the properties and call methods on this object. Gradle nicely makes this `task` object available for use. Behind the nice DSL, we are actually writing a script that creates the build logic in a nice object-oriented way.

Attaching actions to a task

A `Task` object, such as the one created above, does not do much. In fact, there is no action attached to it. We need to attach actions to a `Task` object for Gradle to perform those actions when a task is run.

A `Task` object has a method called `doLast`, which accepts a closure. Gradle ensures that all the closures passed to this methods are executed in the order they were passed:

```
someTask.doLast({
    println "this should be printed when the task is run"
})
```

What we can do now is call `doLast` once more:

```
someTask.doLast({
    println "this should ALSO be printed when the task is run"
})
```

Also, in an alternate syntax:

```
someTask {
    doLast {
        println "third line that should be printed"
    }
}
```

There are multiple ways to add a `doLast` logic to a task, but the most idiomatic, and perhaps a terse way is as follows:

```
someTask << {
    println "the action of someTask"
}
```

Just like the `Project` object, we have the `Task` object on which methods and properties are accessible. However, unlike the `Project` object, it is not implicitly available at the top level in the script, but only inside the task's configuration scope. Also, intuitively, we can say that there will be multiple `Task` objects per `build.gradle`. We will see the various ways to access the `Task` object later.

Task flow control

Tasks within a project may have a dependency on each other. In this section, we will see different kinds of relationships that may exist within tasks of a project.

dependsOn

There are tasks whose execution is dependent on the other task's successful completion. For example, for creating a distributable JAR file, the code should have been compiled first and the "class" files should already exist. In such a case, we don't want the user to explicitly specify all the tasks and their order from the command line, as follows:

```
$ gradle compile dist
```

This is error-prone. We may forget to include one task, or the ordering may become complicated if there are multiple tasks that are dependent on the successful completion of the previous tasks. It is desirable to be able to specify if a:

```
task compile << {
    println 'compling the source'
}

task dist(dependsOn: compile) << {
    println "preparing a jar dist"
}
```

finalizedBy

We can also declare that, if a task is called, it should be followed by another task, even if another task is not explicitly called. This is in contrast to dependsOn, where another task is executed before the called task. In the case of finalizedBy, another task is executed after the execution of the called task:

```
task distUsingTemp << {
  println ("preapring dist using a temp dir")
}

task cleanup << {
  println("removing tmp dir")
}

distUsingTemp.finalizedBy cleanup
```

onlyIf

We can specify a condition and if it is satisfied, the task will be executed:

```
cleanup.onlyIf { file("/tmp").exists() }
```

mustRunAfter and shouldRunAfter

There are times when we just want to order tasks in a particular fashion if this relationship is not exactly the same as `dependsOn`. For example, if we execute the following command:

```
$ gradle build clean
```

Then, unrelated tasks will be executed in the order they were specified on the command line, which in this case doesn't make sense.

In such a case, we may add the following line of code:

```
build.mustRunAfter clean
```

This tells Gradle that, if both the tasks are there in the task graph, then the `build` must run after the `clean` is run. Here, build does not depend on clean.

The difference between `shouldRunAfter` and `mustRunAfter` is that the former is more suggestive to Gradle, but doesn't enforce Gradle to follow the ordering all the time. In the following two cases, `shouldRunAfter` may not be honored by Gradle:

- In the case when it introduces cyclic ordering.
- In the case of parallel execution, when only the `shouldRunAfter` task has not yet successfully completed and other dependencies are satisfied, then `shouldRunAfter` will be ignored.

Creating tasks dynamically

One of the beauties of Gradle is that we can create tasks dynamically as well. What this means is that the name and the logic of task is not completely known while writing the build, but depending on some variable parameter, the tasks will be automatically added to our Gradle project.

Let's try to understand with an example:

```
10.times { number ->
  task "dynamicTask$number" << {
    println "this is dynamic task number # $number "
  }
}
```

In the preceding contrived examples, we are creating and adding ten tasks dynamically to our build. Although all of them just print the task number, the ability to dynamically create and add tasks to our project is extremely powerful.

Setting default tasks

So far, we have always been calling the `gradle` command line interface with the task name(s). This is kind of repetitive in nature, especially during development, and a tool such as Gradle gets us covered:

```
defaultTasks "myTaskName", "myOtherTask"
```

It is wise to set default tasks so that if we don't specify any task name, the set tasks are executed by default.

In the preceding example, running `gradle` from the command line without any arguments runs the default tasks one after another in the sequence specified in the `defaultTasks`.

Task types

The tasks that we have seen so far were ad-hoc in nature. We had to write the code for the task action that needs to be performed whenever the task executes. However, no matter which project we are building, there are many tasks for which the logic of task action need not change if we have the capability to make some configuration changes to the existing logic. For example, when you copy files, only the source, target, and inclusion/exclusion patterns change, but the actual logic of how to copy files from one location to another honoring the inclusion/exclusion patterns stays the same. So, if there are two copy-like tasks required in a project, let's say `copyDocumentation` and `deployWar`, would we really want to write an entire logic to copy the selected files twice?

This would be okay for very small builds (such as the examples in our chapter), but the approach does not scale well. If we keep on writing task actions to perform these mundane operations, then our build scripts will quickly bloat into an unmanageable state.

Custom task type is Gradle's solution to abstract out reusable build logic into custom task classes, which expose the input/output configuration variables on the task object. This helps us tune a typed task to suit our specific needs. This helps us keep the common build logic reusable and testable.

Another problem with ad-hoc task action is that it's imperative in nature. For the sake of flexibility of the tool, Gradle allows us to imperatively script custom logic in build scripts. However, excessive usage of imperative code in our build scripts makes the build script unmaintainable. Gradle should be used in a declarative manner as much as possible. An imperative logic should be encapsulated within a custom task class while exposing the task configuration for the user to configure. In Gradle's terminology, custom task classes are called **enhanced tasks**.

Demystifying Build Scripts

Custom task types act as a template with some sensible defaults for a common build logic. We still need to declare a task in our build, but we just tell Gradle the type of this task and configure the settings of this task type, instead of writing the entire task action block again. Gradle already ships with many custom task types; for example, `Copy`, `Exec`, `Delete`, `Jar`, `Sync`, `Test`, `JavaCompile`, `Zip`, and so on. We can easily write our own enhanced tasks as well. We will very briefly see both the scenarios.

Using task types

We can configure a task that is of type `Copy` using the following syntax:

```
task copyDocumentation(type:Copy) {
from file("src/docs/html")
into file("$buildDir/docs")
}
```

In the preceding example, the first important difference is that we are passing a key `type` with the value as the custom task's class name, which is `Copy` in this case. Also, notice that there is no `doLast` or indirection (`<<`) operator. The closure that we are passing to this task actually gets executed in the configuration phase of build. The method calls inside the closure are delegated to the implicitly available `task` object, which is being configured. We have not written any logic here, but have just provided the configuration to a task whose type is `Copy`. It is always worth taking a look at the available custom tasks before we go ahead with writing ad-hoc task actions.

Creating task types

If we look back now, the code we have been writing for our task actions for our sample tasks was mostly a `println` statement that would print the given message on `System.out`. Now, just imagine that we found `System.out` doesn't fit our bill, and we should rather use text files to print the message from the tasks. We would need to go through all the tasks and change the implementation to write to a file instead of `println`.

There is a better way to handle such changing requirement. We can leverage the capability of the task type here by providing our own task type. Let's put the following code in our `build.gradle`:

```
class Print extends DefaultTask {
  @Input
  String message = "Welcome to Gradle"

  @TaskAction
  def print() {
    println "$message"
  }
```

```
}

task welcome(type: Print)

task thanks(type: Print) {
  message = "Thanks for trying custom tasks"
}

task bye(type: Print)
bye.message = "See you again"

thanks.dependsOn welcome
thanks.finalizedBy bye
```

In the preceding code sample:

- We first created a class (which will be our task type) that extends `DefaultTask`, which is already defined in Gradle.
- Next, we declared a configurable input to our task using `@Input` on the property named `message`. The consumer of our task can configure this property.
- Then, we used the `@TaskAction` annotation on the `print` method. This method is executed when our task is called. It just uses `println` to print the `message`.
- Then, we declared the three tasks; all using different ways to configure our task. Notice the absence of any task action.
- Finally, we applied task flow control techniques to declare task dependencies.

If we run the `thanks` task now, we can see the expected output, as follows:

```
$ gradle -q thanks
Welcome to Gradle
Thanks for trying custom tasks
See you again
```

A few points to note here are as follows:

- If we want to change the implementation of our printing logic, there is only one place where we need to do the change, the `print` method of our custom task class.
- The tasks using task types are used and they work just like any other tasks. They can also have task actions closure using `doLast {}`, `<< {}`, but it is usually not required.

References

The next sections mention some of the useful references for Groovy.

Groovy

There is a plethora of online reference material available for Groovy. We could start at:

- For further reading, refer to Groovy's online documentation at http://www.groovy-lang.org/documentation.html
- More references of Groovy resources are available at https://github.com/kdabir/awesome-groovy

Here is a list of books on Groovy:

- The *Groovy in Action* book is available at https://www.manning.com/books/groovy-in-action-second-edition.
- The *Groovy Cookbook* is available at https://www.packtpub.com/application-development/groovy-2-cookbook.
- The *Programming Groovy 2* book is available at https://pragprog.com/book/vslg2/programming-groovy-2.

Gradle API and DSL used in this chapter

Gradle's official API and DSL documentation is a good place to explore and learn more about various classes discussed in this chapter. These APIs and DSLs are very rich and deserve our reading time.

- Project:
    - The API documentation: http://gradle.org/docs/current/javadoc/org/gradle/api/Project.html
    - The DSL documentation: http://gradle.org/docs/current/dsl/org.gradle.api.Project.html
- Gradle (the interface):
    - The API documentation: http://gradle.org/docs/current/javadoc/org/gradle/api/invocation/Gradle.html
    - The DSL documentation: http://gradle.org/docs/current/dsl/org.gradle.api.invocation.Gradle.html

- Task:
    - The API documentation: `http://www.gradle.org/docs/current/javadoc/org/gradle/api/Task.html`
    - The DSL documentation: `http://www.gradle.org/docs/current/dsl/org.gradle.api.Task.html`

Summary

We started this chapter with a quick feature overview of Groovy language, covering some of the topics that would be helpful for us to understand Gradle's syntax and write better build scripts. Then, we looked at the API that Gradle exposes to our build scripts and how to consume the API via the DSL. We also covered the Gradle build phases. Then, we looked at the way in which tasks can be created, configured, have dependencies between, and run by default.

After reading this chapter, we should be able to comprehend the Gradle DSL, rather than just trying to remember the syntax. We are now in a position to read and understand any given Gradle build file, and we should now be able to write custom tasks with ease.

This chapter might feel a little long and complex. We should take some time out to practise and reread the sections that are not clear and also look up the online references given throughout the chapter. The chapters ahead will be smooth sailing.

5
Multiprojects Build

Now that we are familiar with the build script syntax, we are prepared to handle more complex project structures. In this chapter, we will focus on builds spanning across multiple projects, their interdependencies, and many more things in between.

As the projects code base grows, many times, it is desirable to split it into multiple modules based on layers, responsibilities, artifacts produced, or sometimes even depending on development teams, to effectively break the work down. Whatever is the reason, the reality is big projects are broken down into smaller subprojects sooner or later. Also, a build tool such as Gradle is completely capable of handling the complexity.

The multiproject directory layout

A multiproject (or multimodule, as some prefer to call it) is a group of projects that are logically related to each other and often have the same develop-build-release cycles. The directory structure is important for laying out the strategy for building such projects. Typically, a top-level root project contains one or more subprojects. The root project may contain source sets of its own, may contain only the integration tests that test the integration of the subprojects, or may even act just as a master build without any source and tests. Gradle supports every such configuration.

The arrangement of subprojects relative to the root project may be flat, that is, all the subprojects are the direct children of the root project (as shown in sample 1) or are hierarchical, such that the subproject may also have nested child projects (as shown in sample 2) or any hybrid directory structure.

Multiprojects Build

Let's refer to the following directory structure as sample 1:

```
sample1
├── repository
├── services
└── web-app
```

In sample 1, we see a fictitious example project in which all the subprojects are the direct children of the root project and are siblings of each other. Just for the sake of this example, we broke our app into three subprojects named :repository, :services, and :web-app. As their names suggest, a repository contains the data access code, whereas services is the layer encapsulating the business rules in the form of a consumable API. The web-app contains only the web application-specific code such as controllers and view templates. However, note that the :web-app project may depend on the :services project, which in turn may depend on the :repository project. We will soon see how these dependencies work.

> Do not confuse the multiproject structure with multiple source directories in a single project.

Let's see a relatively more complex structure and call it sample 2:

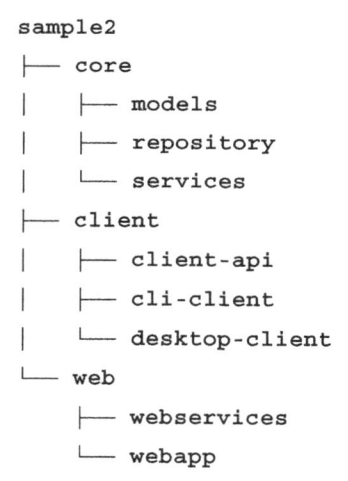

```
sample2
├── core
│   ├── models
│   ├── repository
│   └── services
├── client
│   ├── client-api
│   ├── cli-client
│   └── desktop-client
└── web
    ├── webservices
    └── webapp
```

Our app has now evolved and to cater for more needs, we have added more functionalities to it. We have created more subprojects such as a desktop client for our app and a command-line interface. In sample 2, the root project is split into three projects (groups), which have their own child projects. In this example, every directory can be treated as a project. The purpose of this sample is to only show one of the possible directory structures. Gradle does not impose one directory structure over another.

One might wonder, where do we put all the `build.gradle` files and what goes in them? It depends on our needs and how we want to structure our build. We will answer all these questions shortly after we understand what is `settings.gradle`.

The settings.gradle file

During initialization, Gradle reads the `settings.gradle` file to figure out which projects are to take part in a build. Gradle creates an object of type `Setting`. This happens even before any `build.gradle` is parsed. It is usually placed in the root project parallel to `build.gradle`. It is recommended to put `setting.gradle` in the root project, otherwise we have to explicitly tell Gradle the location to the settings file with the command-line option `-c`. Adding these two files to sample 1's directory structure would gives us something as follows:

```
sample1
├── repository
│   └── ...
├── services
│   └── ...
├── web-app
│   └── ...
├── build.gradle
└── settings.gradle
```

The most common use of `settings.gradle` is to enlist all the subprojects participating in the build:

```
include ':repository', ':services', ':web-app'
```

Also, this is all that is required to tell Gradle that the current build is a multiproject build. Of course, this not the end of the story and there is a lot more that we can do with multiproject builds, but this is the bare minimum and sometimes just enough to get multiproject builds working.

Multiprojects Build

The methods and properties of `Settings` are available in the `settings.gradle` file and are implicitly called on a `Settings` instance just the way the methods of `Project` API are available in the `build.gradle` file, as we saw in the previous chapter.

> Are you wondering why a colon (:) is used before the project name in the preceding section? It denotes the project path relative to the root project. However, the `include` method allows level 1 subproject names to omit the colon. So, the `include` call can be rewritten as follows:
>
>   include 'repository', 'services', 'web-app'

Let's just query the projects by calling the task `projects` from the command line. The `projects` task lists all the projects available in a Gradle build:

```
$ gradle projects
:projects
------------------------------------------------------------
Root project
------------------------------------------------------------

Root project 'sample1'
+--- Project ':repository'
+--- Project ':services'
\--- Project ':web-app'

To see a list of the tasks of a project, run gradle <project-path>:tasks.
For example, try running gradle :repository:tasks.

BUILD SUCCESSFUL
```

> In case of nesting that is more than one level deep, like in sample 2, all the projects must be included in the root project `settings.gradle` with the syntax as follows:
>
>   include 'core',
>   'core:models', 'core:repository', 'core:services',
>   'client' //... so on

We can find more information on `Settings` at the *Settings* DSL documentation (http://www.gradle.org/docs/current/dsl/org.gradle.api.initialization.Settings.html) and the *Settings* API documentation (http://www.gradle.org/docs/current/javadoc/org/gradle/api/initialization/Settings.html).

Organizing build logic in multiproject builds

Gradle gives us the flexibility to create one build file for all projects or individual build file per project; you can also mix and match. Let's start with adding a simple task to our root project's `build.gradle`:

```
task sayHello << {
    println "Hello from multi-project build"
}
```

We are creating a task with an action that just prints a message. Now, let's check what tasks are available on our root project. From the `root` directory, let's call the task `tasks`:

$ gradle tasks

...

Other tasks
----
sayHello

....

No wonder, the `sayHello` task is available on the root project. However, what if we just want to see the tasks available on a subproject? Let's say `:repository`. For a multiproject build, we can call tasks on any nested project using the `gradle <project-path>:<task-name>` syntax or by going into the subproject directory and executing `gradle <task-name>`. So now, if we execute the following code, we won't see the `sayHello` task:

$ gradle repository:tasks

This is because the `sayHello` is only defined for the root project; hence, it is not available on the subproject.

Applying a build logic to all projects

There are times when we want the same tasks to be available on all projects, including the root project. For example, let's imagine a task that just prints the project name. We have four projects, including the root project, and we want to define the same task for every project. Wouldn't it be an overkill if we had to write identical code four times, one for each project? Certainly yes, and that's why Gradle DSL provides a first-class support for declaring common build elements across all projects.

Take a look at the following code snippet, which we will add to our root project's `build.gradle`:

```
allprojects {
    task whoami << {println "I am ${project.name}"}
}
```

Before trying to understand the code snippet, let's run the familiar task again. Firstly, from the root project:

```
$ gradle tasks
...
Other tasks
----------
sayHello
whoami
...
```

Then, from the repository project:

```
$ gradle repository:tasks
...
Other tasks
----------
whoami
...
```

We see the `whoami` task in the repository project as well. Let's uncover the `allprojects` method that made it possible.

The `allprojects` method takes a closure and executes it on the project (object) of the build file and all the subprojects of the current project. So, if `allproject` is defined in the root project, the block gets applied to all the projects one by one, once with each project object as an implicit reference.

Now, let's understand the code snippet. The task that we have declared inside the `allprojects` block (the closure being passed to `allprojects`, to be technically correct) gets applied to all the projects. The task's action prints the name of the project using the `project` object reference. Remember that the `project` object will refer to different projects depending on the project on which the task is being called. This happens because in the configuration phase, the `allproject` block is executed for each project once we have the `project` reference for that project.

The content inside the closure being passed to `allproject` would look exactly like a single-project `build.gradle` file. We can even apply plugins, declare repositories and dependencies, and so on. So, in essence, we can write any build logic that is common to all projects and then it will be applied to all projects. The `allprojects` method can also be used to query the project object in the current build. Refer to the API of the project for more details on `allprojects`.

If we pass the `--all` flag to the `tasks` task, we will see the `whoami` task being present on all the child projects, in addition to the `root` project:

```
$ gradle tasks --all
...
Other tasks
-----------
sayHello
whoami
repository:whoami
services:whoami
web-app:whoami
...
```

If we want to just execute `whoami` on a specific project, let's say `:repository`, it's as simple as the following command:

```
$ gradle -q repository:whoami
I am repository
```

When we execute `whoami` without any project path:

```
$ gradle -q whoami
I am root
I am repository
I am services
I am web-app
```

[93]

Wow, Gradle goes an extra mile to ensure that the child project tasks with the same name are also executed when we execute the task from the parent project. This comes in very handy when we think about tasks such as `assemble`, where we actually want all the subprojects to assemble, or test, which tests the root and also the subprojects.

However, what about executing a task only on the root project? Indeed, a valid scenario. Remember the absolute task path:

```
$ gradle -q :whoami
I am root
```

The colon makes all the difference. Here, we are referring to `whoami` of the `root` project only. No other task matches the same path. For example, repository's `whoami` has a path `repository:whoami`.

Now, `cd` in the `repository` directory and then execute the `whoami`:

```
$ gradle -q whoami
I am repository
```

So the task execution is context-sensitive. Here, by default, Gradle assumes that the task has to be called on the current project only. Nice, isn't it?

Let's add a little more dynamic code to our existing `build.gradle` file:

```
allprojects {
  task("describe${project.name.capitalize()}") << {
    println project.name
  }
}
```

Here, depending on the project name, we are setting the task name to be `describe`, prefixed to the project name. So all projects get their tasks, but the name won't be the same. We add an action that just prints the project name. If we execute the `tasks` on our project now, we can see the task names include the project name:

```
$ gradle tasks
...
Other tasks
-----------
describeRepository
describeSample1
describeServices
describeWeb-app
sayHello
whoami
...
```

Although the example is very trivial, we learn a few things. Firstly, the `allprojects` blocks are additive as most of the other methods in Gradle. We added the second `allprojects` block and both worked just fine. Secondly, the task name can be dynamically assigned, for example, using the project name.

Now, we can call any of the `describe*` tasks from the project root. Also, as we might guess, the task name is unique; we don't need to prepend the project path:

```
$ gradle -q describeServices
services
```

Let's `cd` into the `repository` directory and list tasks:

```
$ gradle -q tasks
...
Other tasks
-----------
describeRepository
whoami
```

We see only the applicable tasks for the current project, which is `repository`.

Applying build logic to subprojects

Let's continue further with our example. Here, the root project will not have any source sets as all the Java code is going to be in one of the three child projects. Hence, wouldn't it be wise to apply a `java` plugin to only child projects? This is exactly where the `subprojects` method comes into the picture, that is, when we want to apply some build logic only on subprojects without affecting the parent project. Its usage is similar to `allprojects`. Let's just apply the `java` plugin to all subprojects:

```
subprojects {
  apply plugin: 'java'
}
```

Now, running `gradle tasks` should show us the tasks added by the `java` plugin as well. Although it might appear that these tasks are available on the root project, it's actually not so. Check the output of `gradle -q tasks --all` in this case. The tasks being there on the child project can be called from the root project, but this does not mean they are present on the root project. The tasks added by the `java` plugin will only be available on subprojects, whereas tasks such as help tasks will be available on all projects.

Dependency on subprojects

In the beginning of the chapter, we mentioned that a subproject might depend on another subproject(s) just the way it can depend on the external library dependency. For example, the services project's compilation depends on the repository project, which means we need the compiled classes from the repository project to be available on the compilation classpath of the services project.

To achieve this, we can, of course, create a build.gradle file in the services project and put the dependency declaration there. However, just for the sake of showing an alternate way, we will put this declaration in the root project's build.gradle.

Unlike allprojects or subprojects, we need a finer mechanism to configure only a single project from the root project's build.gradle. As it turns out, it is very easy using the project method. This method accepts a closure just like the allprojects and subprojects methods in addition to the project name on which the closure will be applied. In the configuration phase, the closure is executed on that project's object.

So, let's add this to the root project's build.gradle:

```
project(':services') {
  dependencies {
    compile project(':repository')
  }
}
```

Here, we are configuring dependencies only for the services project. In the dependencies block, we declare that the :repository project is the compile time dependency for the services project. This is more or less similar to the external library declaration; instead of the library name in the group-id:artifact-id:version notation, we used project(:sub-project) to refer to a subproject.

We had also said that the web-app project depends on the services project. So this time, let's use web-app's own build.gradle to declare this dependency. We will create a build.gradle file in the web-app directory:

```
root
├── build.gradle
├── settings.gradle
├── repository
├── services
└── web-app
    └── build.gradle
```

As this is a project-specific build file, we can just add the `dependencies` block as we would in any other project:

```
dependencies {
  compile project(':services')
}
```

Now, let's visualize the dependencies of the web project, using the `dependencies` tasks:

```
$ gradle -q web-app:dependencies


------------------------------------------------------------
Project :web-app
------------------------------------------------------------

archives - Configuration for archive artifacts.
No dependencies

compile - Compile classpath for source set 'main'.
\--- project :services
     \--- project :repository

default - Configuration for default artifacts.
\--- project :services
     \--- project :repository

runtime - Runtime classpath for source set 'main'.
\--- project :services
     \--- project :repository

testCompile - Compile classpath for source set 'test'.
\--- project :services
     \--- project :repository

testRuntime - Runtime classpath for source set 'test'.
\--- project :services
     \--- project :repository
```

Gradle shows us the dependencies of the `web-app` under various configurations. Also, we can clearly see that Gradle understands the transitive dependency; hence, it shows `web-app` transitively dependent on `repository` through `services`. Note that we have not actually declared any external dependencies (such as `servlet-api`) in any of the projects, otherwise they would also show up here.

It is worth taking a look at the variations of the `configure` methods on the `project` object in order to filter and configure selected projects. More information on the `configure` method can be found at https://docs.gradle.org/current/javadoc/org/gradle/api/Project.html.

Summary

In this short chapter, we learned that Gradle supports flexible directory structure for complex project hierarchies and allows us to choose the right structure for our build. We then looked at the importance of `settings.gradle` in the context of mutliprojects build. We then saw various ways of applying a build logic to all projects, subprojects, or only a single project. Finally, took a small example of inter-project dependencies.

This is all we need to worry about in terms of the Gradle syntax. Now the next chapters will majorly focus on the functionalities that various plugins add to our builds and how we can configure them.

6
The Real-world Project with Gradle

Until now, we have discussed about building the Java project, web project, Gradle life cycle, and multi-module feature of Gradle. As we know, before Gradle, there were many other build tools in the market, out of which the most popular ones are Ant and Maven. Since many project build scripts were already written in these two build tools. In this chapter, we will discuss different migration strategies to migrate the projects existing build scripts from Ant, Maven, to Gradle. Along with this, we will also focus on integrating Gradle build script to Continuous Integration tools like Jenkins and generating Java docs for the code.

Migrating from an Ant-based project

Ant is one of the initial and most popular build tools, which made build and deployment processes much simpler as compared to other native script-based build tools. Still, you can find many projects that use Ant build script to build the project. Ant was developed on the philosophy of imperative programming model, which tells the system what to do and also how to do it. Thus, you have the benefit of controlling each and every action or step of your build script. The following is the sample Ant build script to build any Java project. Here, we are considering only minimal required tasks to build a Java project, since our purpose is to discuss the strategies to migrate from Ant scripts to Gradle scripts:

```
<project name="Ant build project" default="createJar">
  <target name="clean" description="clean the existing dirs">
    <delete dir="build"/>
    <delete dir="dist"/>
  </target>
```

```xml
<target name="compile" description="compile the source"
  depends="clean">
  <mkdir dir="build"/>
  <mkdir dir="dist"/>
  <mkdir dir="build/classes"/>
  <javac srcdir="src" destdir="build/classes"/>
</target>
<target name="createJar" depends="compile" description="create the
  jar">
  <jar jarfile="dist/JavaProject-1.0.jar" basedir="build/classes"/>
</target>
</project>
```

Here, we have defined three targets such as `clean`, `compile`, and `createJar`, which will delete the directories, create the directories, compile the Java file present in source directories, and finally create the `.jar` file, respectively. There are three different strategies that a developer can follow in order to migrate the build scripts from Ant to Gradle, as follows:

- Importing an Ant file
- Using AntBuilder API
- Rewriting Ant tasks to Gradle tasks

We will discuss each of them with an example.

Importing an Ant file

The very first and simplest approach for migration is to directly import your Ant script file into a Gradle script. Consider the following structure:

```
C:\GRADLE\CHAPTER6
|   build_import.gradle
|   build.xml
|
└───src
    └───main
        └───java
            └───ch6
                    SampleJava.java
```

Here, the project name is Chapter6, the Java source directory is src/main/java, and the Ant build script file is build.xml. The source code of build.xml is mentioned above. Now, as a part of the migration, create the build_import.gradle file with the following contents:

```
ant.importBuild 'build.xml'
```

That is all. Yes, we have successfully migrated the Ant build script to Gradle script. Now, try to execute the following command:

```
> gradle -b build_import.gradle createJar
:clean
:compile
:createJar
BUILD SUCCESSFUL
Total time: 3.045 secs
```

After executing this, you can find the build/classes and dist directory in the project directory, and dist contains the JavaProject.jar file.

Using AntBuilder API

Another approach to migrate is using AntBuilder API. By default, Gradle provides an AntBuilder object ant to the user. The user can use this object directly in the Gradle script to call the Ant tasks. The following is the sample code of the build_antbuilder.gradle file using AntBuilder API:

```
task cleanDir << {
  ant.delete(dir:"build")
  ant.delete(dir:"dist")
}

task compileSrc(dependsOn:'cleanDir') << {
  ant.mkdir(dir:"build/classes")
  ant.mkdir(dir:"dist")
  ant.javac(srcdir:"src", destdir:"build/classes",
  includeantruntime:"false")
}
task createJar(dependsOn:'compileSrc') << {
  ant.jar(destfile: "dist/JavaProject-1.0.jar", basedir:"build/
  classes")
}
```

Here, you can see we have used different Ant tasks such as `mkdir`, `javac`, `jar`, and so on, as a method of an `ant` object. Now, execute the following command:

```
> gradle -b build_antbuilder.gradle createJar
:cleanDir
:compileSrc
:createJar
BUILD SUCCESSFUL
Total time: 3.437 secs
```

Here also, you will find the same output, that is, it will create the `build/classes` directory in which you can find class files and the `dist` directory in which you can find the `.jar` file.

Rewriting Ant tasks to Gradle tasks

This is the final approach. Using this approach rather than using an `ant` object, you actually rewrite the complete build logic or functionality using the actual Gradle tasks. One simple approach to follow this strategy is that the user first needs to logically understand the complete flow file written in Ant and then convert it into a Gradle script step by step. For all the targets defined in Ant, the user can create tasks in Gradle, and for all the tasks defined in Ant, the user can use Gradle features to replicate the same behavior. Gradle provides different standard plugins to support most of the steps of the build requirement. A plugin has its own life cycle, and with the help of plugins, the user can avoid rewriting lot of boiler-plate scripts for a common build functionality. One such plugin is the `java` plugin. We have already seen the `java` plugin details in *Chapter 2, Building Java Projects*. If we want to migrate this Ant script to Gradle script in order to build a Java project, the user can simply use a `Java` plugin and job is done.

Consider the `build.gradle` file with the following contents:

```
apply plugin:'java'
```

If a developer follows the default conventions of a `java` plugin, he only needs to write this one line to build a Java project, and on executing the `gradle build` command, all the required steps would be done such as compiling code, executing unit test cases, and preparing a `.jar` file. However, this is not the case always; many legacy projects do not follow the conventions and they might have their own conventions. The `gradle` plugin provides the flexibility to configure the plugin based on the project's need. We will rewrite the Ant script into Gradle script in the following sample code:

```
apply plugin:'java'

task cleanDir << {
  delete "build"
```

```
    delete "dist"
}

task createDirs(dependsOn:'cleanDir') << {
  def classes = file("build/classes")
  def dist = file("dist")
  classes.mkdirs()
  dist.mkdirs()

}
compileJava {
  File classesDir = file("build/classes")
  FileTree srcDir = fileTree(dir: "src")
  source srcDir
  destinationDir classesDir
}
task createJar(type: Jar) {
  destinationDir = file("dist")
  baseName = "JavaProject-1.0"
  from "build/classes"
}
createJar.dependsOn compileJava
compileJava.dependsOn createDirs
```

The preceding code snippet shows how you can rewrite the Ant script to Gradle script. On executing the `gradle createJar` command, it will generate the same output which was generated by following above migration strategies.

Migrating from a Maven project

Maven, one of the another build tool, which got most popularity after Ant and it also came with dependency management solution to the problem that the users were facing in Ant. The first problem in Ant was imperative programing where user has to write lots of boiler plate code. Another problem was dependency management. Ant does not have any in-built dependency management solution (Ant later integrated with Ivy for dependency management). A user has to write each and every JAR file path in the build file that it needs to download, and in case of transitive dependencies, it is too complex for the user to identify each and every dependent JAR and mention the JAR name in the build file. Also, in case of version conflicts, it consumes lots of a developer's efforts. Maven came with the declarative programing model and in-built dependency management solution. Gradle is also built on the top of these principles; thus, migrating from Maven to Gradle seems very comfortable for the user.

Like Ant migration, Gradle does not provide any import feature or in-built Maven object. A user needs to rewrite the Maven script to the Gradle script. The following are some of the concepts that will help you to smoothly migrate from Maven to Gradle:

- Plugin declaration
- Common conventions
- Dependency management
- Repositories configuration

Let's move towards the explanation of these concepts:

- **Plugin declaration**: The plugin is the key driver for both Maven and Gradle functionalities. Same as Maven plugins, Gradle also packages most of its functionalities into plugins. In Maven, a user includes the plugin in the following XML format:

    ```
    <plugin>
      <artifactId>pluginName</artifactId>
      <version>2.3.2</version>
    </plugin>
    ```

    To include a plugin, the user only needs to write the `apply plugin` statement as follows:

    ```
    apply plugin: '<plugin name>'
    ```

- **Common conventions**: In both Maven and Gradle, a plugin always comes with some common conventions for its functionalities. For example, if a user includes a `java` plugin, the common convention is that the source code location should be `src/main/java`, test code location should be `src/test/java`, and so on. If a user includes a plugin and follows the same convention, then he can avoid writing any boiler-plate code that could save both his time and effort.

- **Dependency management**: Both Maven and Gradle come with in-built dependency management features. A user does not need to bother about each and every individual JAR required for the project. He just needs to mention the first-level dependency in the project, the rest all is taken care by the build tool.

    In Maven, a user can mention the dependency in the following format:

    ```
    <dependency>
      <groupId> org.apache.logging.log4j</ groupId>
      <artifactId>log4j-core </ artifactId>
      <version>1.2</version>
      <scope>compile</scope>
    </dependency>
    ```

To define the dependency in Gradle, a user has to use the following syntax:

```
dependencies{
compile(' org.apache.logging.log4j: log4j-core:1.2')
}
```

What scope is to Maven, the dependency configuration is to Gradle. You might have observed the scope attribute in Maven and dependency configuration attributes in Gradle. In Maven, scope identifies at which phase of build dependency needs to be downloaded. In Gradle, dependency configurations fulfill the same need.

- **Repositories configuration**: Whenever we talk about dependencies, the first thing that comes into mind is the repository. This is the location from where you download dependencies. The following is the code snippet that can help you mention the repository location in Maven:

```
<repositories>
  <repository>
    <id>repository_1</id>
    <name>custom Name</name>
    <url> http://companylocalrepository.org </url>
  </repository>
</repositories>
```

In Gradle, you can mention the repository using the following syntax:

```
repositories {
  maven {
    url "http://companylocalrepository.org"
  }
}
```

As we have seen, both Maven and Gradle follow the same philosophy for building any project. The main difference is Maven uses XML that is good at structure, but can be a pain while configuring the build script, whereas Gradle uses Groovy script that is a DSL and offers great flexibility while managing and altering the default behavior.

Publishing artifacts

Building a software does not make much sense unless you publish your software to some common repositories so that, if needed, it can be reused by other software or projects. We have discussed the repositories while downloading the dependencies. The other aspect of repositories is uploading the build outcome (JAR, WAR, EAR, and so on) to some common location so that it could be downloaded by other developers. The different plugins in Gradle provide an automated way to publish the default artifacts of the plugin. For example, a `java` plugin provides a task to upload a JAR file, a `war` plugin provides a task to upload a WAR file, a `scala` plugin provides a task to upload a JAR file, and so on. A user just needs to configure the *upload repository* location. If a user does not want to upload the default build artifact or a user wants to upload some custom artifacts, he can easily customize Gradle tasks to upload the other artifacts and also as per his custom requirements.

As we have seen, a `java` plugin provides different configurations such as compile, testCompile, runtime, and so on, to download JAR for a specific scope. To upload artifacts, Gradle provides one additional configuration, **archives**. A user can configure the artifact in archives configuration, and using the `uploadArchive` task, he can upload the artifacts to a repository.

The following is the sample example of the build file (`build_uploadArtifact.gradle`) to upload a JAR file generated by a `java` plugin:

```
apply plugin: 'java'
version=1.0
repositories {
  mavenCentral()
}
dependencies {
  compile ('log4j:log4j:1.2.16')
}
uploadArchives {
  repositories {
    maven {
      credentials {
        username "user1"
        password "user1"
      }
      url "http://company.private.repo"
    }
  }
}
```

You can execute the `gradle -b build_uploadArtifact.gradle uploadArchives` command to upload the artifacts. As a part of life cycle, it will build and upload the artifacts.

In the preceding example, the `uploadArchives` task uploads the artifact to a repository (mentioned in the URL). If it is a secured repository, you can provide a username and password, or else ignore it. You have noticed that we have not mentioned archives here, so what would get uploaded? As we have already discussed, a `java` plugin builds the JAR file, a `war` plugin builds the WAR file, and so on. Thus, the default artifact generated by a plugin would be uploaded by default as a part of the `uploadArchives` task. We will see another example as to how to upload your custom artifact.

The following is the `build_uploadCustom.gradle` file:

```
apply plugin: 'java'
archivesBaseName="JavaProject" // to customize Jar Name
version=1.0
repositories {
  mavenCentral()
}
def customFile= file('configurations.xml')
task customZip(type: Zip) {
  from 'src'
}
artifacts {
  archives customFile
  archives customZip
}
uploadArchives {
  repositories {
    flatDir {dirs "./tempRepo"}
  }
}
```

Now, execute the `gradle -b build_uploadCustom.gradle uploadArchives` command:

```
>gradle -b build_uploadCustom.gradle uploadArchives
:customZip UP-TO-DATE
:compileJava UP-TO-DATE
:processResources UP-TO-DATE
:classes UP-TO-DATE
:jar UP-TO-DATE
```

```
:uploadArchives

BUILD SUCCESSFUL

Total time: 4.014 secs
```

Here, you can find that a new directory `tempRepo` is created after executing the build script. This contains all the above artifacts (ZIP, JAR, and XML files) that are published by the Gradle script.

In the preceding example, we have covered the following two cases:

- Uploading a custom file (a XML and ZIP file along with the default artifact)
- Uploading to a local file system (not on a central repository)

If you configure any other custom file (JAR, WAR, or any other file) to the archives, it will also get uploaded to the repository. Here, we have configured two additional files, one `.xml` file and one `.zip` file along with the default Java artifact. If you want to share your artifacts with your team mates and at the same time do not want to upload the artifact to the repository, unless it passes integration tests, Gradle gives you the flexibility to upload the file to a local file system using `flatDir`.

Gradle recently introduced a `maven-publish` plugin to have more control over the publishing process. It gives you many additional flexibilities along with the default publish tasks. A user can modify the POM file, publish multiple modules, and so on.

> You can find more details at https://docs.gradle.org/current/userguide/publishing_maven.html.

Continuous Integration

Continuous Integration (CI) is one of the most popular buzzwords you can read everywhere. As is apparent from its name, CI is the process of integrating the code base each time; whenever any one makes commits to the repository. It compiles the code, run the unit test cases and prepare the build. One of the benefits a user gets here is, if there are compile issues and integration issues, a user can figure out at early stages, rather than it being too late. The following is the generic workflow the CI tool follows:

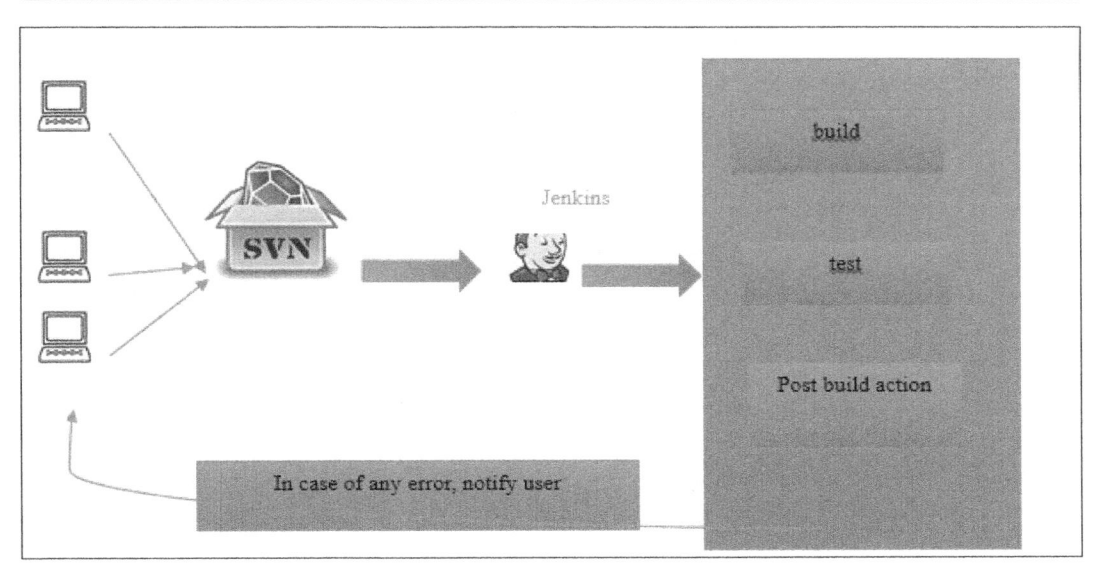

Figure 6.1

How does Gradle fit into this flow? To plan the build and deployment automation solution for any software, we need a different set of tools to work together to achieve the common goal. Jenkins is one of the integration tools that helps to integrate the complete workflow. It also works on the concept of plugins; you can add different plugins to Jenkins (for example, Gradle, Git, Svn, and so on) as per your need and configure them to plan the automation flow.

Here, we are assuming that you have installed Jenkins. You can install a **Gradle plugin** by navigating to **Manage Jenkins | Manage Plugins | Search for Gradle**.

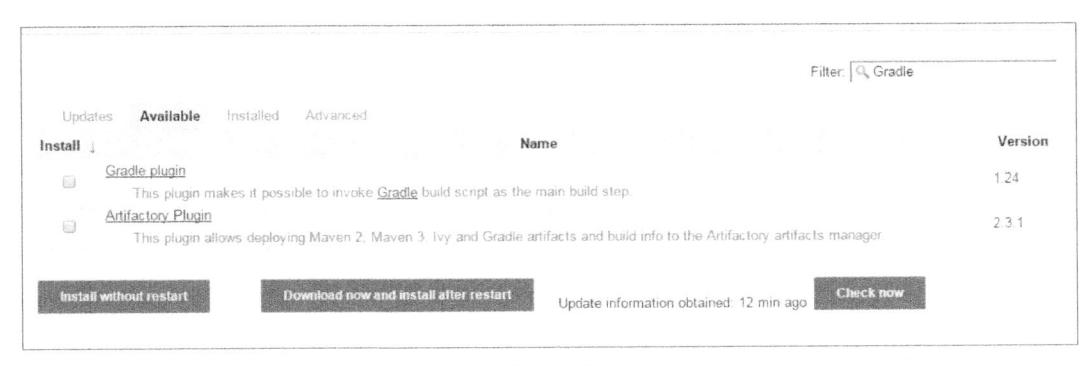

Figure 6.2

The Real-world Project with Gradle

Once a plugin is installed, you can configure jobs in Jenkins using the following screenshot:

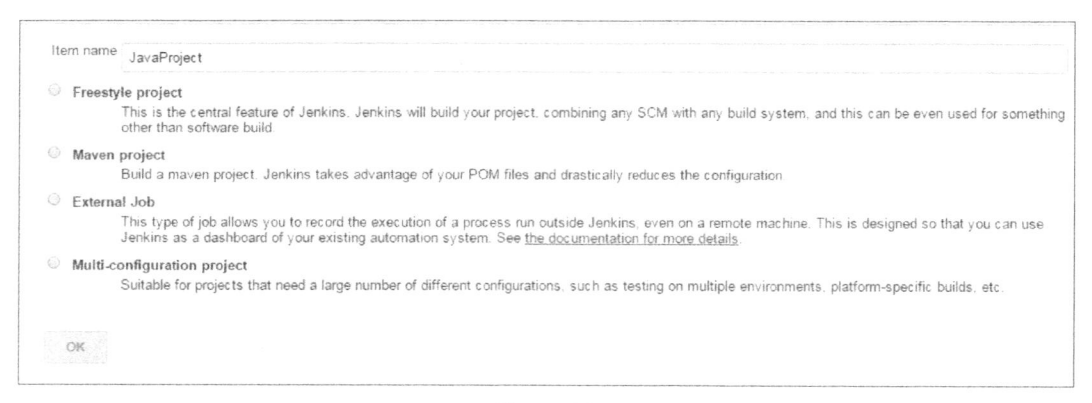

Figure 6.3

Under project configuration screen, you need to configure the repository path. By default, Jenkins provides CVS and SVN plugins. If you need any other repository (perforce or Git), you can add the respective plugins. After repository configuration, you need to configure the **Build Triggers**. It allows you to trigger build periodically or, if you want to build on every commit, you can choose **Poll SCM**. Now, it is time to configure your build script that will build your project.

Under the **Build** menu, you can choose **Invoke Gradle script**:

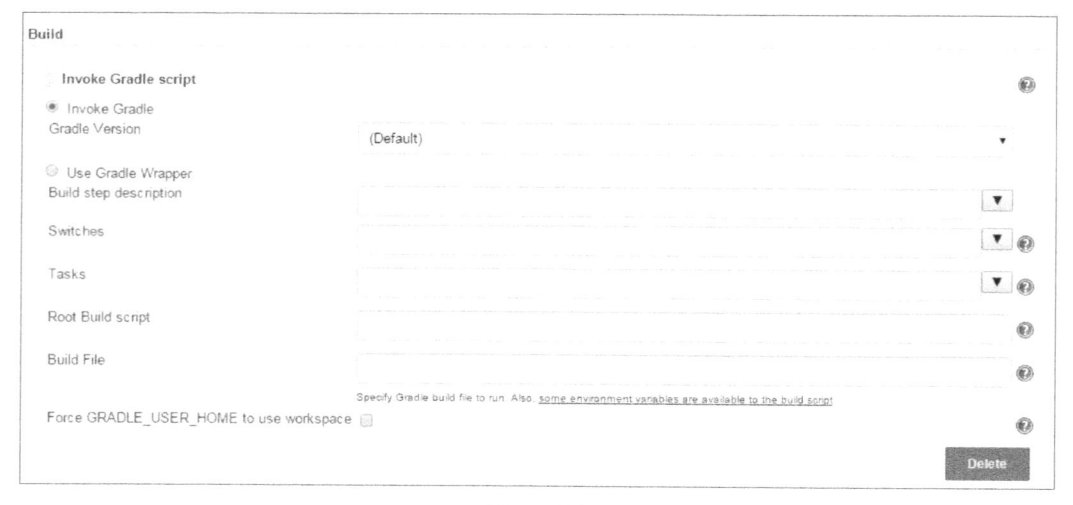

Figure 6.4

If you are using the default build file name `build.gradle`, there is no need to configure the build file. Under **Task**, you can mention the name of the task you want to execute. For example, if you want to build the project, you can mention `build` in the text box.

Once the configuration is done, you can click on **Build Now** on the left menu to build the project. Once done, click on the respective build number and it will display **Console Output** on the main screen:

```
Console Output

Started by user anonymous
Building in workspace C:\Gradle\Chapter6
[Gradle] - Launching build.
[Chapter6] $ cmd.exe /C '"gradle.bat build -b C:\Gradle\Chapter6\build.gradle && exit %%ERRORLEVEL%%"'
:cleanDir
:createDirs
:compileJava
:processResources UP-TO-DATE
:classes
:jar
:assemble
:compileTestJava UP-TO-DATE
:processTestResources UP-TO-DATE
:testClasses UP-TO-DATE
:test UP-TO-DATE
:check UP-TO-DATE
:build

BUILD SUCCESSFUL

Total time: 4.419 secs
Build step 'Invoke Gradle script' changed build result to SUCCESS
Finished: SUCCESS
```

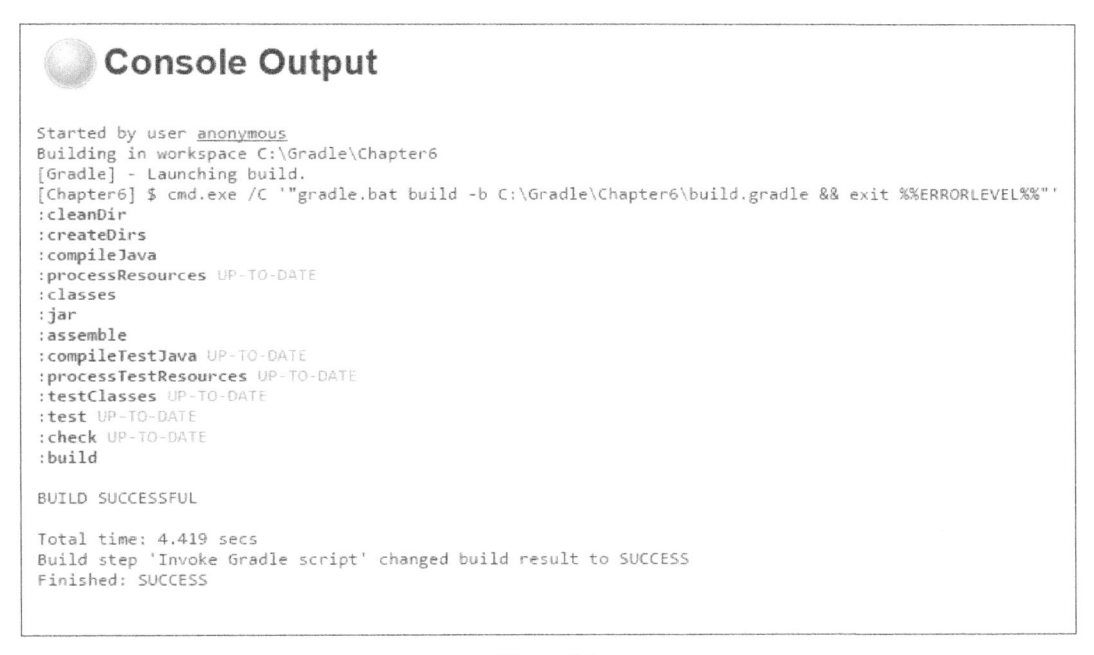

Figure 6.5

Generating documentation

Documentation is one of the important part of development life cycle, which does not get enough attention from developers. If code is not properly documented, it always increases the maintenance efforts and also it takes time for the new team member to understand the code, if the code lacks the documentation. When you apply **Java plugin** to your build file, Gradle provides you a `javadoc` task. By default, Gradle generates the initial documentation for your code, even if the user does not mention any **Javadoc** in the file.

Consider the following Java sample code:

```
package ch6;
public class SampleTask {
  public static void main(String[] args) {
    System.out.println("Building Project");

  }
  public String greetings(String name) {
    return "hello "+name;
  }
}
```

Now, try to execute the following command:

```
> gradle clean javadoc
:clean
:cleanDir
:createDirs
:compileJava
:processResources UP-TO-DATE
:classes
:javadoc

BUILD SUCCESSFUL

Total time: 4.341 secs
```

This command will generate the basic Java docs at `<project> \build\docs\javadoc`.

As per requirements, you can add your own tags (`@description`, `@param`, and so on) and details to the above class and get the updated Java docs.

Summary

In this chapter, we discussed different migration strategies from existing build tools to Gradle, which could be very handy for users who are planning to migrate their existing Ant and Maven scripts to Gradle. We also discussed how to publish artifacts to repositories, which is a key functionality of any build tool, which help the users to always fetch the latest artifacts from the repositories. We discussed CI framework with the help of Jenkins and how Gradle fits into this flow, while automating the build and deployment solution. Finally, we discussed how to generate documents for the Java code.

In the next chapter, we will be discussing how to integrate TestNG with Gradle, which would help the user to run test cases as a part of the Gradle build. We will also be discussing integration testing strategies and Gradle integration with code analysis and code coverage tools.

7
Testing and Reporting with Gradle

In this chapter, we will cover four different topics: testing with TestNG, integration testing, code coverage with JaCoCo, and code analysis with Sonar. In *Chapter 2, Building Java Projects*, we already discussed unit testing with JUnit. In this chapter, we'll cover another widely used testing tool, TestNG. Code coverage and code quality are the other two important aspects in **test-driven development** (**TDD**). In today's agile development process, developers need continuous feedback on the code developed by them. Code quality tools help us to achieve this goal. Often, these tools are integrated with the **Continuous Integration** (**CI**) systems so that these reports are created on a daily basis (may be even after each commit), shared among different teams, and even be persisted for future analysis. In this chapter, we will be focusing only on the Gradle aspects of different tools. We will mainly cover different Gradle plugins that support these features.

Testing with TestNG

Working with TestNG is similar to the JUnit integration that we discussed in *Chapter 2, Building Java Projects*. The very first step is to create the build file with TestNG dependencies and configure the test closure. The following build file adds the TestNG library as the `testCompile` dependency and in the test closure, we added a `testng.xml` file to execute the test cases. In this section, we will briefly discuss the use of `testng.xml`:

```
apply plugin:'java'

repositories {
  mavenCentral()
}
```

```
dependencies {
  testCompile 'org.testng:testng:6.8.21'
}

test {
  ignoreFailures = true
  useTestNG(){
    suites("src/test/resources/testng.xml")
  }
}
```

> However, you can read more about TestNG configuration at http://testng.org/doc/documentation-main.html.

In our example, we have created three test cases named as `verifyMapSize`, `verifyMapNotNull`, and `addEvenNumbers`. These test cases are grouped as `Smoke` and `Integration` test cases. If you execute a Gradle test command, all the three test cases will be executed and the test report will be created in the `build/reports/tests` directory. The look and feel of the report is similar to the JUnit report that we saw earlier. The actual TestNG report is created in the `test-output/` directory in the project home directory. Both JUnit and TestNG generate their own different report formats, but Gradle reconciles them into a standard look and feel:

```
package com.packtpub.ge.ch7;

import java.util.HashMap;

import org.testng.Assert;
import org.testng.annotations.AfterMethod;
import org.testng.annotations.BeforeClass;
import org.testng.annotations.Test;

public class HashTest {

  private HashMap<Integer,String> hm;

  @BeforeClass(alwaysRun = true)
  public void setup(){
    hm = new HashMap<Integer, String>();
  }

  @AfterMethod(alwaysRun = true)
  public void cleantask(){
```

```
      hm.clear();
    }

    @Test(groups = "Smoke")
    public void verifyMapSize(){
      Assert.assertEquals(hm.size(), 0);
      hm.put(1, "first");
      hm.put(2, "second");
      hm.put(3, "third");
      Assert.assertEquals(hm.size(), 3);
    }

    @Test(groups = "Smoke")
    public void verifyMapNotNull(){
      Assert.assertNotNull(hm);

    }

    @Test(groups = "Integration")
    public void addEvenNumbers(){
      hm.put(2, "second");
      hm.put(4, "fourth");
      Assert.assertEquals(hm.size(), 2);
    }


}
```

A TestNG test case can be executed from a command line, Ant file, Gradle script, Eclipse plugin, or a TestNG test suite file. TestNG suite files provide a flexible mechanism control for the test execution. In a test suite file, you can define test classes, tests, test group names, listener information, and so on.

We have created a sample `testng.xml` file in the `src/test/resource` folder. The file has some important information. The **listener configuration** to create a report format, a **test group** declaration as `Smoke`, and a test class named `com.packtpub.ge.ch7.HashTest`.

Gradle doesn't force you to put `testng.xml` in the `src/test/resources`, and we're just doing this as a means to keep it organized:

```
<!DOCTYPE suite SYSTEM "http://testng.org/testng-1.0.dtd" >
<suite name="Suite1" verbose="1" >
  <listeners>
    <listener class-name="org.testng.reporters.EmailableReporter" />
```

```xml
    </listeners>
    <test name="Smoke Test">
    <groups>
      <run>
        <exclude name="Integration"  />
        <include name="Smoke"  />
      </run>
    </groups>
    <classes>
      <class name="com.packtpub.ge.ch7.HashTest">
      </class>
    </classes>
    </test>
</suite>
```

As we have only included test cases that are marked as Smoke, the TestNG invoked only two test cases, verifyMapNotNull and addEvenNumbers, when we executed the gradle test command. The following figure shows the TestNG report that is created in the `<Project_Home>/ test-output/` directory:

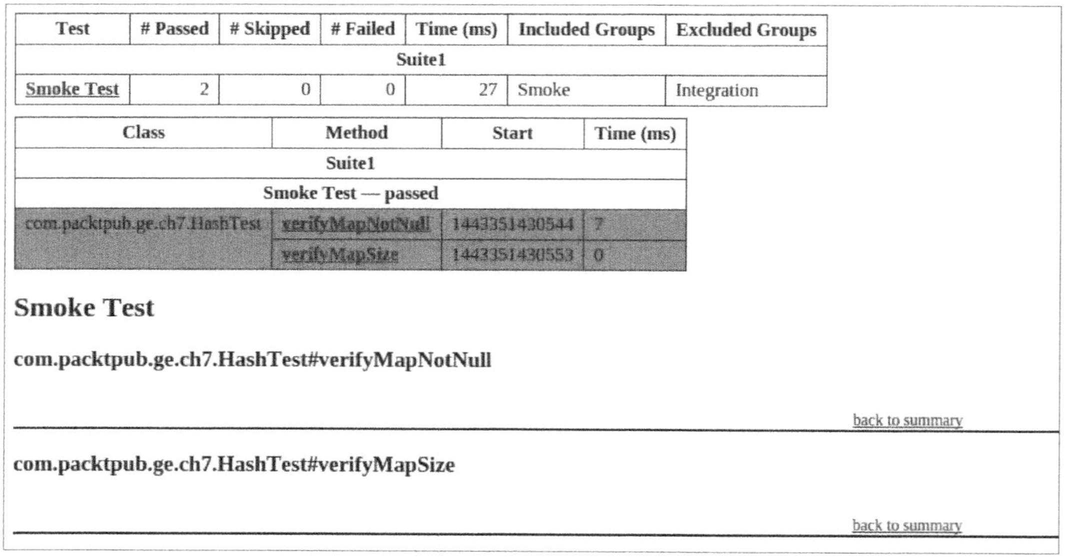

Test	# Passed	# Skipped	# Failed	Time (ms)	Included Groups	Excluded Groups
Suite1							
Smoke Test	2	0	0	27	Smoke	Integration

Class	Method	Start	Time (ms)
Suite1			
Smoke Test — passed			
com.packtpub.ge.ch7.HashTest	verifyMapNotNull	1443351430544	7
	verifyMapSize	1443351430553	0

Smoke Test

com.packtpub.ge.ch7.HashTest#verifyMapNotNull

back to summary

com.packtpub.ge.ch7.HashTest#verifyMapSize

back to summary

Figure 7.1

Integration testing

Unit testing is one of the key step in software development life cycle. It is one of the first checks to verify the code quality. Most of the basic functionalities can be tested with unit test cases. They are quick and take little time to execute. We discussed both JUnit framework and TestNG framework to unit test the code. The next step in the quality check process is integration testing. As by general definition of unit testing, you divide your code into small units and test them independently, which is good when you are developing your code independently. Once you commit the code and integrate the code with other developers, you need another level of testing, which is known as integration testing. It verifies the communication between different components working together as expected or not. Your test reports might give 100 percent success results in unit testing, but unless and until you perform integration testing, you cannot be assured of the functionality of the software as a whole.

We have already seen Gradle support for unit testing and how Gradle provides conventions to write your test classes in different directory structures and tasks to execute the test cases. Gradle does not differentiate between unit testing and integration testing, if we talk in terms of the convention it provides. To enable integration testing along with unit testing in Gradle, you need to customize the Gradle to enable both. Consider the following hierarchy for your project source code:

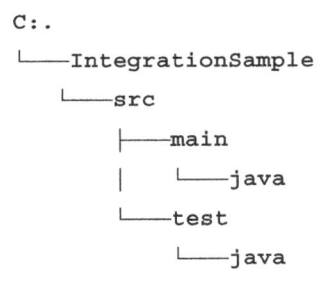

```
C:.
└───IntegrationSample
    └───src
        ├───main
        │   └───java
        └───test
            └───java
```

This is the standard folder structure you create for your source and test code. You create `src/test/java` to store your unit test cases. Now, if you want to add integration test cases to your project, you can merge the integration test cases in the same directory structure; however, this would not be a good design—since you might want to execute the unit test case each time you build your project and might want to execute the integration test biweekly or weekly—as it might consume more time depending on the project complexity and size. Thus, rather than merging the integration tests to your unit test cases' directory structure, we recommend you to create a separate directory structure, `src/integrationTest/java`, for integration test cases, and you can configure the same in your Gradle build scripts.

The following will be the updated directory structure to store the integration test cases:

```
C:.
└───IntegrationSample
    └───src
        ├───integrationTest
        │   └───java
        ├───main
        │   └───java
        └───test
            └───java
```

Once you have created the directory structure, you need to configure this in your Gradle build script. The updated build script would be as follows:

```
apply plugin: 'java'
sourceSets {
   integrationTest {
       java.srcDir file('src/integrationTest/java')
       resources.srcDir file('src/integrationTest/resources') // to add the resources
   }
}

task runIntegrationTest(type: Test) {
   testClassesDir = sourceSets.integrationTest.output.classesDir
   classpath = sourceSets.integrationTest.runtimeClasspath
}
```

Here, we have added one extra configuration, `integrationTest`, to add the integration test cases. To execute the integration tests, we have also defined one task, `runIntegrationTest`, which is of type `Test` and configured the `testClassesDir` and classpath attributes. Once we have added additional `sourceSets` to the build script, the `java` plugin automatically adds two new dependency configurations to your build script `integrationTestCompile` and `integrationTestRuntime`.

Execute the following command to check for the current dependencies:

```
> gradle dependencies
------------------------------------------------------------
Root project
------------------------------------------------------------
```

```
.......
compile - Compile classpath for source set 'main'.
No dependencies
integrationTestCompile - Compile classpath for source set 'integration
test'.
No dependencies
integrationTestRuntime - Runtime classpath for source set 'integration
test'.
No dependencies
.........
BUILD SUCCESSFUL
Total time: 3.34 secs
```

Here, `integrationTestCompile` can be used to configure dependencies required to compile the test cases and `integrationTestRuntime` can be used to configure dependencies required to execute the test cases. As you can see, no dependencies are explicitly configured for integration test cases. You can configure them under dependencies closure:

```
dependencies {
// other configuration dependencies
integrationTestCompile 'org.hibernate:hibernate:3.2.3.ga'
}
```

We do not want to execute the integration tests each time we build the project. Thus, to execute the integration test, you need to explicitly execute the following command:

> **gradle runIntegrationTest**

This will invoke the `runIntegrationTest` task and will execute the integration test cases. If you want to execute these test cases each time you build your code, you can link this task with other tasks using `dependsOn` or any other dependency attributes.

Code coverage

There are so many coverage tools available for source code analysis such as EMMA, Corbatura, JaCoCo, and so on. In this section, we'll cover Gradle integration with JaCoCo to find the source code analysis.

Before we get started, we need to understand what code coverage is and why it is important in the test-driven development.

Code coverage is a metric that we can use to check how much of the source code was tested. Higher code coverage means a greater percentage of our code has been tested. Code coverage is typically done in the unit testing cycle. During code coverage, a developer must ensure that different logical paths in the source code have been tested and verified to achieve better code coverage.

Here, it is important to understand that the code coverage is not directly related to code quality. High code coverage does not guarantee that the quality code has been written. A developer must use static code analysis tools such as PMD (https://pmd.github.io/) to find the quality of the code. Another point to remember is that, even with 100 percent of code coverage, there is no guarantee that a complete bug-free code has been written. Thus, many developers argue that this not a right metric to be considered for the code quality or unit test. However, 70-80 percent code coverage is considered to be a good number for healthy code coverage.

In Gradle, the code coverage tool, JaCoCo, can be applied to a project like any other plugin:

```
apply plugin: 'jacoco'
```

Our `build.gradle` file has the following content. We have created a few TestNG test cases to test the functionalities of the source code. We have also configured a test task to be dependent on the `jacocoTestReport` task. This is to make sure that test cases are executed before running and creating the test coverage reports:

```
apply plugin: 'java'
apply plugin: 'jacoco'

repositories {
  mavenCentral()
}

dependencies {
  testCompile 'org.testng:testng:6.8.8'
}

test{
    systemProperty "url",System.properties['url']
    useTestNG()
}

jacocoTestReport.dependsOn test
```

By default, the report will be created in the `<build dir>/reports/jacoco/test/html` directory and an HTML report file will be generated. For example, we have created a simple POJO `User.java` file with the getter and setter methods. Also, we have created a few unit test cases to verify the functionalities. The two sample test cases are as follows:

```java
@Test
public void userEmailTest() {
  User user1 = new User("User2", "User2 user2", "user2@abc.com");
  Assert.assertEquals(user1.getEmail(), "user2@abc.com");
}

@Test
public void userIdTest() {
  User user1 = new User();
  user1.setUserId("User3");
  user1.setName("User3 user3");
  user1.setEmail("user3@abc.com");
  Assert.assertEquals(user1.getName(), "User3 user3");
  Assert.assertEquals(user1.getUserId(), "User3");
}
```

Next, we can execute the `jacocoTestReport` task to generate the code coverage report:

```
> gradle clean jacocoTestReport
:clean
:compileJava
:processResources UP-TO-DATE
:classes
:compileTestJava
:processTestResources UP-TO-DATE
:testClasses
:test
:jacocoTestReport

BUILD SUCCESSFUL

Total time: 7.433 secs
```

In the coverage report, you can observe that all the methods of the Java class were tested unit tests. You can further drill down following the links in the report that shows the line coverage on the source code. The source code is marked in green and red to display what is covered and what is not tested. The following figure (*Figure 7.2*) shows the code coverage statistics for the `User.java` class:

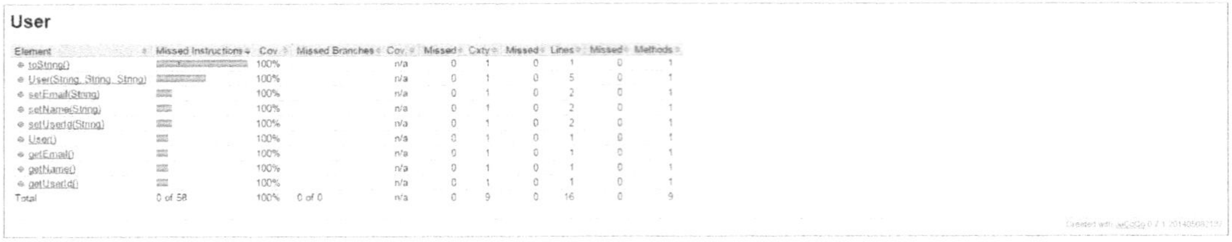

User

Element	Missed Instructions	Cov.	Missed Branches	Cov.	Missed	Cxty	Missed	Lines	Missed	Methods
toString()		100%		n/a	0	1	0	1	0	1
User(String, String, String)		100%		n/a	0	1	0	5	0	1
setEmail(String)		100%		n/a	0	1	0	2	0	1
setName(String)		100%		n/a	0	1	0	2	0	1
setUserId(String)		100%		n/a	0	1	0	2	0	1
User()		100%		n/a	0	1	0	1	0	1
getEmail()		100%		n/a	0	1	0	1	0	1
getName()		100%		n/a	0	1	0	1	0	1
getUserId()		100%		n/a	0	1	0	1	0	1
Total	0 of 58	100%	0 of 0	n/a	0	9	0	16	0	9

Figure 7.2

By default, an HTML report file is generated in the `build/reports/jacoco/test/html` directory. Also, the default version of the `jacoco` plugin can be modified by modifying the `jacoco` extension as follows:

```
jacoco {
    toolVersion = "<Required-Version>"
    reportsDir = file("Path_to_Jacoco_ReportDir")
}
```

Similarly, the report can be customized by configuring the `jacocoTestReport` task as follows:

```
jacocoTestReport {
    reports {
        xml.enabled false
        html.destination "<Path_to_dircectory>"
    }
}
```

Code analysis reports

Sonar is one of the most popular quality management tools that gives a complete analysis of a project in terms of lines of code, documentation, test coverage, issues, and complexities. As a developer, we are mainly interested in the following areas:

- Duplicate lines of code
- Lacking comments in the source code, especially in public APIs
- Not following coding standards and best practices
- Finding code complexity
- Code coverage produced by unit tests

In this section, we will discuss Gradle integration with Sonar. The only prerequisite is, the Sonar server should be installed and running.

A prerequisite to run Sonar is to have Java installed on the box. Once prerequisites are met, you can install Sonar in just three simple steps as follows:

1. Download the distribution from `http://www.sonarqube.org/downloads/` and unzip it.
2. Open a console and start the Sonar server:
    - On Windows platforms, start `$SONAR_HOME\bin\windows-x86-32\StartSonar.bat`
    - On other platforms, start `$SONAR_HOME/bin/[OS]/sonar.sh`
3. Go to `http://localhost:9000`.

To run `sonar-runner` plugin, we just need to apply the plugin `sonar-runner` and configure it to connect to the Sonar server.

Create the build file `build.gradle` for your project with the following contents:

```groovy
apply plugin: 'groovy'
apply plugin: "sonar-runner"

repositories {
    mavenCentral()
}

version = '1.0'
repositories {
    mavenCentral()
}

sonarRunner {
  sonarProperties {
    property "sonar.host.url", "http://<IP_ADDRESS>:<PORT>"
    property "sonar.jdbc.url",
    "jdbc:h2:tcp://<IP_ADDRESS>:<PORT>/sonar"
    property "sonar.jdbc.driverClassName", "org.h2.Driver"
    property "sonar.jdbc.username", "sonar"
    property "sonar.jdbc.password", "sonar"
  }
}
```

The above configuration is self-explanatory. You need to add configurations such as Sonar URL, DB URL, and JDBC driver details, and our build file is ready.

Testing and Reporting with Gradle

The next step is to run the `sonarRunner` task for code analysis. After successful execution of this task, you will find the report hosted on the Sonar server:

```
>gradle clean sonarRunner
:clean
:compileJava
:processResources UP-TO-DATE
:classes
:compileTestJava
:processTestResources UP-TO-DATE
:testClasses
:test
:sonarRunner
SonarQube Runner 2.3
Java 1.7.0_51 Oracle Corporation (64-bit)
Windows 7 6.1 amd64
INFO: Runner configuration file: NONE
INFO: Project configuration file: <Project_Home>\UserService\build\tmp\sonarRunner\sonar-project.properties
INFO: Default locale: "en_IN", source code encoding: "windows-1252" (analysis is platform dependent)
INFO: Work directory: <Project_Home>\UserService\build\sonar
INFO: SonarQube Server 3.7.4
...
...
```

Now, you can open `http://localhost:9000/` to browse the projects. This page is the default dashboard page, which shows the details of all the projects. You can find your project and browse through the details. The details will be displayed as follows:

Chapter 7

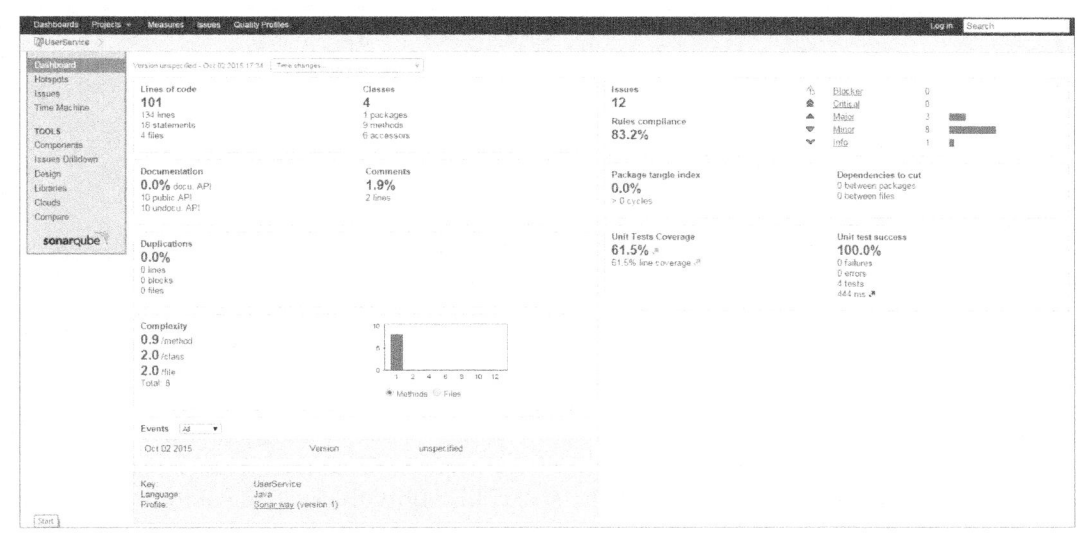

Figure 7.3

You can again further verify the details of each metric, just by following the links provided in the project home page. For example, the following figure displays the source code-related metrics in the Sonar. It provides details such as code complexity, lines of code, methods, documentation, and so on:

Figure 7.4

> You can find more on Sonar at http://docs.sonarqube.org/display/SONAR/Documentation/.

Summary

In this chapter, we discussed the testing and reporting aspects of Gradle. We started our discussion with TestNG and also discussed how we can configure Gradle to support the integration test cases separate from unit test cases. Then, we discussed code coverage with JaCoCo and, finally, we talked about Sonar integration with Gradle.

In the next chapter, we will discuss how to organize the build logic in build scripts and plugins. We'll explore how to modularize plugin code so that it can be shared across multi-project Gradle build. We'll also explore how to create a custom plugin in Gradle.

Organizing Build Logic and Plugins

Plugins are one of the major building blocks of Gradle, which we have not discussed much until now. You have seen different standard plugins such as Java, Eclipse, Scala, and so on, which comes with a set of defined tasks. Developers just include the plugin, configure the required tasks, and leverage the functionalities. In this chapter, we will get an overview of what a plugin is, how you can group tasks to a plugin, how you can extract the plugin logic from a build file to buildSrc, and also how to create a standalone plugin.

Extracting build logic to buildSrc

Plugins are nothing but the group of tasks with specific orders and default configurations, which are created to provide a certain functionality. For example, java plugin contains tasks that provide the functionality to build a Java project, scala plugin contains tasks to build Scala projects, and so on. Although Gradle provides many standard plugins, you can also find different third-party plugins to fulfil the project's need. There might always be a case when you are not able to find the desired functionality with the existing plugins and would like to create a new one for your custom requirement. We will see the different ways in which a developer can create a plugin and use it.

The very first plugin that a user can create is in the build file itself. The following is the sample code of a plugin, which a developer can write in build.gradle and use it:

```
apply plugin: CustomPlugin

class CustomPlugin implements Plugin<Project> {
  void apply(Project project) {
    project.task('task1') << {
```

```
        println "Sample task1 in custom plugin"

    }
    project.task('task2') << {
        println "Sample task2 in custom plugin"

        }
    }
}
task2.dependsOn task1
```

Here, we have created a plugin in the build file itself. This is the beauty of Gradle script. You can also write a class in the Gradle file. To create a custom plugin, you need to create a Groovy class that implements the `Plugin` interface. You can write a plugin even in Java or any other JVN language. Since Gradle build scripts are written in Groovy, we have used Groovy to write the plugin implementation. All the tasks that you want to implement, you need to define inside the `apply` method. We have defined two tasks, `task1` and `task2`. Also, we have defined the life cycle as a relationship between the two tasks. If a developer calls `task1`, only `task1` will be executed. If you execute `task2`, both `task1` and `task2` will get executed. Try to execute the following command:

```
> gradle task2
:task1
Sample task1 in customer plugin
:task2
Sample task2 in custom plugin

BUILD SUCCESSFUL
Total time: 2.206 secs
```

> To use a plugin in the build file, you always need to use `apply plugin:<plugin name/plugin` class (if a plugin is implemented in the same script or in the `buildSrc` directory).

This is one of the simple ways in which a developer can define a custom plugin. However, if we follow the design principles, it is not a good practice to mix the build logic and custom logic into the same file. It would be difficult to maintain the code and it might also increase the maintenance efforts. We will always recommend you to write plugin code separate from the build logic. To achieve this, Gradle provides two different ways as follows:

- Extract plugin code to `buildSrc`
- Independent plugin

To extract plugin code to `buildSrc`, Gradle recommends you to create a `buildSrc` directory inside the project directory and keep the plugin code there. The following is the folder hierarchy for the same:

```
C:./Gradle/Chapter8/CustomPlugin1
│   build.gradle
│
└───buildSrc
    └───src
        └───main
            └───groovy
                └───ch8
                        CustomPlugin.groovy
```

Here, we have created a separate `buildSrc` directory; inside that, we kept the plugin code in the `CustomPlugin.groovy` file. Move the preceding Groovy class from the `build.gradle` file into this file. Include the package statement at the top. You also need to import the `org.gradle.api.*`. Your `CustomPlugin.groovy` file will look as follows:

```
package ch8
import org.gradle.api.*
class CustomPlugin implements Plugin<Project> {
// Plugin functionality here
}
```

The `build.gradle` file contents will be as follows:

```
import ch8.CustomPlugin
apply plugin: CustomPlugin
```

You just need to import the package and add the apply `plugin` statement. All the background work of compiling the class and including the class into classpath at the runtime, will be performed by Gradle. Now, try to execute the following command:

```
> gradle task1
:buildSrc:compileJava UP-TO-DATE
:buildSrc:compileGroovy UP-TO-DATE
:buildSrc:processResources UP-TO-DATE
:buildSrc:classes UP-TO-DATE
:buildSrc:jar UP-TO-DATE
:buildSrc:assemble UP-TO-DATE
:buildSrc:compileTestJava UP-TO-DATE
```

```
:buildSrc:compileTestGroovy UP-TO-DATE
:buildSrc:processTestResources UP-TO-DATE
:buildSrc:testClasses UP-TO-DATE
:buildSrc:test UP-TO-DATE
:buildSrc:check UP-TO-DATE
:buildSrc:build UP-TO-DATE
:task1
Sample task1 in custom plugin

BUILD SUCCESSFUL

Total time: 3.374 secs
```

Here, you can see that Gradle performed the compile and build task for your custom plugin code, and now you just need to execute the tasks that are part of your custom plugin. Gradle also allows you to configure your custom plugin in a build file. You can set a dependency between the tasks or add more functionality to the tasks in the build file itself, rather than updating your plugin code again and again. If you want to add some more features for task1, you can do it as follows:

```
task1.doLast {
println "Added more functionality to task1"
}
task2.dependsOn task1
```

Now, if you try to execute task1, it will append the preceding statement.

In this way, you can separate the build logic from the build.gradle file to a separate class file under buildSrc directory. If you have a multi-project build, the plugin defined in the root project buildSrc can be reused by all the subprojects' build files. You do not need to define a separate plugin for each sub-projects. This process has still one limitation. It does not allow you to use this plugin for other projects. Since it is tightly coupled with the current project, you can use this plugin only with the same project or the sub-projects defined in the root project. To overcome this, you can plug out the plugin code into a standalone plugin and package it into a JAR file, which you can publish to a repository so that it can be reused by any projects. In the next section, we will discuss the standalone plugin.

The first plugin

To make the plugin reusable for all the other projects, Gradle allows you to separate the plugin code and package it in a JAR file. You can include this JAR file in any projects in which you want to reuse this functionality. You can create the standalone project in Java or Groovy. We will proceed with Groovy. You can use any editor (Eclipse, NetBeans, or Idea) to create a plugin. Since our main purpose is to show you how to create a standalone plugin, we will not go into the details of the editor. We will use a simple text editor. To proceed with the standalone plugin, separate the above `buildSrc` code into an independent directory. You can name it `CustomPlugin`. So, the directory structure will be as follows:

```
C:/Gradle/Chapter8/CustomPlugin.
|   build.gradle
|
└───src
    └───main
        └───groovy
            └───ch8
                    CustomPlugin.groovy
```

You might be surprised to know why we are creating a `build.gradle` file here. With this `build.gradle`, we will package the plugin code into a JAR file. Now, the question arises as to how you will include this plugin into other build files. You need a **plugin ID** for this plugin. To add a plugin ID to your plugin, you need to create a property file inside the `src/main/resources/META-INF/gradle-plugins` directory. The name of the properties file will be your plugin ID. Here, we will add the `customplugin.properties` file in the above directory. The content of this file will be as follows:

```
implementation-class=ch8.CustomPlugin

Your build file content would be.

apply plugin: 'groovy'
version = '1.0'
dependencies {
  compile gradleApi()
  compile localGroovy()
}
```

Organizing Build Logic and Plugins

To compile Groovy code, you need to include the preceding two statements in compile configurations. Since we are using a plain vanilla Groovy class here, we have not added any other dependency JARs. If your plugin code has a dependency on any other third-party JARs, you can include them in the dependency and configure the respective repositories.

Now, we will build the plugin as follows:

```
> gradle clean build
:clean
:compileJava UP-TO-DATE
:compileGroovy
:processResources
:classes
:jar
:assemble
:compileTestJava UP-TO-DATE
:compileTestGroovy UP-TO-DATE
:processTestResources UP-TO-DATE
:testClasses UP-TO-DATE
:test UP-TO-DATE
:check UP-TO-DATE
:build

BUILD SUCCESSFUL
Total time: 4.671 secs
```

You can find the JAR file inside `<project>/build/libs/CustomPlugin-1.0.jar`.

You can publish this plugin JAR to your organization's internal repositories so that any other projects can directly download it from there and use it. Now, we will create another project and will refer to this plugin JAR into that project.

Create a new directory, `SampleProject`, and add `build.gradle` to the project. Now, a question arises as to how will your `build.gradle` refer to `SamplePlugin`. For this, you need to mention the location of the `SamplePlugin` JAR in `buildscript closure` and add dependency to this JAR in the `dependencies` closure.

Chapter 8

The content of your `build.gradle` will be as follows:

```
buildscript {
repositories {
   flatDir {dirs "../CustomPlugin/build/libs/"}
}
dependencies {
classpath group: 'ch8', name: 'CustomPlugin',version: '1.0'
}
}
apply plugin: 'customplugin'
```

Here, we are using a `flat file repository`, thus, referring to the custom plugin JAR using the `flatDir` configuration. We recommend you to use the organization's local repository; thus, it can be centrally accessed by any of the organization's projects. In the dependencies closure, we are referring to the `CustomPlugin` JAR file. This is the prerequisite to use any plugin. Finally, we are adding the `apply plugin` statement and mentioning the plugin name in single quotes.

> The plugin name is the name of the property file you create in the `src/main/resources/META-INF/gradle-plugins` directory.

Now, you can execute the build file using the following command:

> **gradle task1**

:task1
Sample task1 in custom plugin

BUILD SUCCESSFUL

Total time: 2.497 secs

Organizing Build Logic and Plugins

Configuring plugins

So far, we have seen how to create a standalone custom plugin and include it in another project build file. Gradle also allows you to configure plugin properties and customize them as per your project's need. You have already learned how you can customize the source code location and test code location in a `java` plugin. We will see an example of how you can replicate the same behavior in your custom plugin. To define plugin properties, you need to create one additional `extension` class and register the class into your `plugin` class. Let's say we want to add the `location` property to the plugin. Create the `CustomPluginExtension.groovy` class as follows:

```
package ch8
class CustomPluginExtension {
def location = "/plugin/defaultlocation"
}
```

Now, register this class to your `plugin` class:

```
class CustomPlugin implements Plugin<Project> {
  void apply(Project project) {
     def extension = project.extensions.create("customExt",CustomPlugi
nExtension)

  project.task('task1') << {
       println "Sample task1 in custom plugin"
       println "location is "+project.customExt.location
  }
}
}
```

Now, build the plugin again so that your changes are part of the latest plugin JAR file and then try to execute `build.gradle` of `SampleProject`:

```
> gradle task1
:task1
Sample task1 in custom plugin
location is /plugin/defaultlocation


BUILD SUCCESSFUL


Total time: 2.79 secs
```

Here, you can see the default value on the command line output. If you want to change this field to some other value, add `customExt closure` to your `SampleProject build.gradle` file with a different value configured for the location:

```
buildscript {
repositories {
  flatDir {dirs "../CustomPlugin/build/libs/"}
}
dependencies {
  classpath group: 'ch8', name: 'CustomPlugin',version: '1.0'
}
}
apply plugin: 'customplugin'

customExt {
  location="/plugin/newlocation"
}
```

Now try to execute `task1` again:

```
> gradle task1
:task1
Sample task1 in custom plugin
location is /plugin/newlocation

BUILD SUCCESSFUL
Total time: 5.794 secs
```

Here, you can observe the update value for the location attribute.

Summary

In this chapter, we discussed one of Gradle's main building blocks, plugins. A plugin helps to organize and modularize the functionality and also helps to package a set of related tasks and configurations. We also discussed the different ways of creating custom plugins, from writing the plugin code in the build file itself to creating a standalone plugin JAR file and reusing it in different projects. In the last section, we also covered how you can configure the plugin's existing properties and customize them as per your project's requirement.

Before concluding this book in the next chapter, we will be discussing how you can build Groovy and Scala projects with the help of Gradle. Also, as this is a mobile age, where all the traditional software or web applications are now moving to apps, we will also be discussing building Android projects.

9
Polyglot Projects

We are living in an era where one language is not enough. Developers are expected to be polyglot programmers and choose the right tool for a job. While it is always a subjective decision, we try to select languages and ecosystems based on various parameters such as execution speed, developer productivity, available libraries and resources, a team's comfort level with the language, and many more.

When we are already carrying the cognitive load of working with different languages, Gradle turns out to be our good friend, as we don't have to change our build tool even if we are building projects in other languages. We can even use multiple languages in the same project and Gradle orchestrating the build for the entire project. Apart from the array of JVM-based languages, Gradle also supports C, C++, Objective C and others to produce native applications as well. Gradle is also an official build tool for the Android platform. The list of supported languages is on the rise. Apart from official plugins, there are many community-supported language plugins.

Although throughout the book we have focused primarily on Java as the language, we could have very well used Groovy or Scala to write the examples. The `java` plugin (along with the `java-base` plugin, which is applied by the `java` plugin to the project) provides the basic functionality for the JVM-based projects. Language specific plugins such as `scala` and `groovy` extend the `java` plugin to support common idioms in a consistent manner. So, once we have used the `java` plugin, we are already familiar with what `sourceSet` is, how `configuration` works, how to add library dependencies, and so on, and this knowledge is readily useful when we use these language plugins. In this chapter, we will see how we can easily add more spice to Java projects by adding Groovy or Scala to the mix.

The polyglot application

For the code example, in this chapter, let's build a simple **Quote of the Day** service that returns a quote based on the day of the year. Since we might have fewer quotes in our store, the service should repeat the quotes in a cyclic fashion. Again, as usual, we will try to keep it as simple as possible to focus more on build aspects rather than the application logic. We will create two separate Gradle projects to implement the exact same functionality, once in Groovy then in Scala.

Before going into language-specific details, let's start with defining the QotdService interface, which just declares only one method, getQuote. The contract is, as long as we pass the same date, we should get the same quote back:

```
package com.packtpub.ge.qotd;

import java.util.Date;

interface QotdService {
  String getQuote(Date day);
}
```

The logic to implement getQuote can use the Date object in any manner, such as using the entire date including the time for determining the quote. However, for the sake of simplicity, we will use only the day component of the Date object in our implementations. Also, because we want our interface to be open for future implementations, we let getQuote take a Date object as the parameter.

This interface is a Java file that we will have in both projects. This is just to demonstrate the integration of Java and Groovy/Scala sources in one project.

Building Groovy projects

Let's first implement the QotdService interface in Groovy. Also, we will write some unit tests to make sure that the functionality works as expected. To start the project, let's create the directory structure as follows:

```
qotd-groovy
├── build.gradle
└── src
    ├── main
    │   ├── groovy
```

```
|   |       └── com
|   |           └── packtpub
|   |               └── ge
|   |                   └── qotd
|   |                       └── GroovyQotdService.groovy
|   └── java
|       └── com
|           └── packtpub
|               └── ge
|                   └── qotd
|                       └── QotdService.java
└── test
    └── groovy
        └── com
            └── packtpub
                └── ge
                    └── qotd
                        └── GroovyQotdServiceTest.groovy
```

The `src/main/java` directory is the default directory for Java sources. Similarly, `src/main/groovy` is used by default to compile Groovy source files. Again, it is just a convention, and the source directories' path and name can be easily configured via `sourceSets`.

Let's first write the build script for our Groovy project. Create a `build.gradle` file in the project root with the following content:

```
apply plugin: 'groovy'

repositories {
  mavenCentral()
}

dependencies {
  compile 'org.codehaus.groovy:groovy-all:2.4.5'
  testCompile 'junit:junit:4.11'
}
```

Building Groovy project is as simple as building a Java project. Instead of applying the `java` plugin, we apply the `groovy` plugin, which automatically applies the `java` plugin for us. Apart from applying the plugin, we also need to add Groovy as a library dependency so that it is available for compilation and is also available at runtime. We also add `junit` in the `testCompile` configuration so it is available for unit tests. We declare Maven central as the repository to be used, but this can be changed to any valid repository configuration that can serve our project's dependencies.

> Gradle build script is a Groovy DSL, and parts of Gradle are written in Groovy. However, like any other library that Gradle itself depends on at runtime, Groovy is not implicitly available to the project that we are building. Hence, we must explicitly declare Groovy as a project dependency, depending on whether we are using Groovy in production or test sources.

Groovy plugin takes care of compiling Java source files in the project as well. Let's implement the `QotdService` interface in Groovy:

```
package com.packtpub.ge.qotd

class GroovyQotdService implements QotdService {
  List quotes

  GroovyQotdService(List quotes) {
    this.quotes = quotes
  }

  @Override
  String getQuote(Date day) {
    quotes[day[Calendar.DAY_OF_YEAR] % quotes.size()]
  }
}
```

The implementation of service accepts a list of quotes in a constructor. The `getQuote` method gets quote by the index in the list. To ensure that the computed index always stays within the range of the quote's size, we get the modulus of the day of the year and the list's size.

To test the service, let's write very basic JUnit test cases in Groovy:

```
package com.packtpub.ge.qotd

import org.junit.Before
```

```
import org.junit.Test

import static org.junit.Assert.assertEquals
import static org.junit.Assert.assertNotSame


public class GroovyQotdServiceTest {

  QotdService service
  Date today, tomorrow, dayAfterTomorrow

  def quotes = [
    "Be the change you wish to see in the world" +
      " - Mahatma Gandhi",
    "A person who never made a mistake never tried anything new" +
      " - Albert Einstein"
  ]

  @Before
  public void setup() {
    service = new GroovyQotdService(quotes)
    today = new Date()
    tomorrow = today + 1
    dayAfterTomorrow = tomorrow + 1
  }

  @Test
  void "return same quote for same date"() {
    assertEquals(service.getQuote(today), service.getQuote(today))
  }

  @Test
  void "return different quote for different dates"() {
    assertNotSame(service.getQuote(today),
      service.getQuote(tomorrow))
  }

  @Test
  void "repeat quotes"() {
    assertEquals(service.getQuote(today),
      service.getQuote(dayAfterTomorrow))
  }
}
```

We prepare the test data in setup, and each test case makes sure the contract of the quote service is maintained. As the quote's list contains only two quotes, they should repeat every alternate day.

We can run the tests from the command line using the following code:

```
$ gradle test
```

Building Scala projects

Following the last section, most of this section would be very predictable from the application build's standpoint. So let's quickly go through the gist of it. The directory structure is as follows:

```
qotd-scala
├── build.gradle
└── src
    ├── main
    │   ├── java
    │   │   └── com/packtpub/ge/qotd
    │   │       └── QotdService.java
    │   └── scala
    │       └── com/packtpub/ge/qotd
    │           └── ScalaQotdService.scala
    └── test
        └── scala
            └── com/packtpub/ge/qotd
                └── ScalaQotdServiceTest.scala
```

All Scala source files are read from src/main/scala and src/test/scala, unless configured using sourceSets. This time, the only plugin that we need to apply is the scala plugin, which just like the groovy plugin, implicitly applies the java plugin to our project. Let's write the build.gradle file for this project:

```
apply plugin: 'scala'

repositories {
  mavenCentral()
}

dependencies {
  compile 'org.scala-lang:scala-library:2.11.7'
```

```
    testCompile 'org.specs2:specs2-junit_2.11:2.4.15',
      'junit:junit:4.11'
}
```

Here, we have to provide `scala-library` as a dependency. We also added `specs2` as a dependency for the test configuration. We are using JUnit runner for the tests.

> The `specs2` is a popular Scala testing library, which supports both unit and acceptance testing and the BDD/TDD style of writing tests. More information is available at http://etorreborre.github.io/specs2/.

Moving on to the service's Scala implementation, we can implement it as follows:

```
package com.packtpub.ge.qotd

import java.util.{Calendar, Date}

class ScalaQotdService(quotes: Seq[String]) extends QotdService {

  def getQuote(day: Date) = {
    val calendar = Calendar.getInstance()
    calendar.setTime(day)

    quotes(calendar.get(Calendar.DAY_OF_YEAR) % quotes.size)
  }
}
```

The implementation is not very idiomatic Scala, but that's out of scope of this book. The class takes the quotes `Seq` in the constructor and implements the `getQuote` method in a similar fashion to the Groovy counterpart.

Now that the service is implemented, let's verify that it honors the semantics of `QotdService` by writing unit tests. For brevity, we will cover only the important test cases:

```
package com.packtpub.ge.qotd

import java.util.{Calendar, Date}

import org.junit.runner.RunWith
import org.specs2.mutable._
import org.specs2.runner.JUnitRunner

@RunWith(classOf[JUnitRunner])
```

```scala
class ScalaQotdServiceTest extends SpecificationWithJUnit {

  def service = new ScalaQotdService(Seq(
    "Be the change you wish to see in the world" +
      " - Mahatma Gandhi",
    "A person who never made a mistake never tried anything new" +
      " - Albert Einstein"
  ))

  val today = new Date()
  val tomorrow = incrementDay(today)
  val dayAfterTomorrow = incrementDay(tomorrow)

  "Quote service" should {
    "return same quote for same day in multiple invocations" in {
      service.getQuote(today) must be(service.getQuote(today))
    }

    "return different quote for different days" in {
      service.getQuote(today) must not be (
        service.getQuote(tomorrow))
    }

    "repeat quote if total quotes are less than days in year" in {
      service.getQuote(today) must be(
        service.getQuote(dayAfterTomorrow))
    }
  }

  def incrementDay(date: Date) = {
    val cal = Calendar.getInstance()
    cal.setTime(date)
    cal.add(Calendar.DATE, 1)
    cal.getTime
  }
}
```

The task to run test cases is just the same as the Groovy counterpart. We can run tests using the following code:

```
$ gradle test
```

Joint compilation

In the preceding examples in this chapter, we declared an interface in Java and implemented it in Groovy and Scala respectively. It was possible because the classes compiled by the `java` plugin are available to Groovy and Scala classes.

If we want a Java class to have access to Groovy or Scala classes for its compilation, then we must compile the Java source file using the **joint compilation** supported by the respective plugin. Both the `groovy` and `scala` plugins support joint compilation and can compile Java sources.

For referencing Groovy classes in a Java class, the easiest way is to move the corresponding Java source file into `src/main/groovy` (or in any of the Groovy `srcDirs` configured for `sourceSets`), and the Groovy compiler makes Groovy classes available to the Java class while compilation. The same goes for Scala joint compilation. We can put the Java files, which need Scala classes for their compilation, in any of the Scala `srcDirs` (`src/main/scala` by default).

References

The detailed official documentation for language plugins, discussed in this chapter, can be found at the following URLs:

- **Java plugin**: https://docs.gradle.org/current/userguide/java_plugin.html
- **Groovy plugin**: https://docs.gradle.org/current/userguide/groovy_plugin.html
- **Scala plugin**: https://docs.gradle.org/current/userguide/scala_plugin.html

The links to the official documentation for various languages and other plugins shipped with Gradle can be found at the following URL:

https://docs.gradle.org/current/userguide/standard_plugins.html

Summary

We took a simple example problem and implemented a solution in Groovy and Scala to demonstrate how Gradle makes polyglot project development easy. Instead of going into language and plugin-specific details and differences, we tried to focus on the commonality and consistency that Gradle brings to the table.

Index

A

Ant-based project, migrating from
  about 99, 100
  AntBuilder API, using 101, 102
  Ant file, importing 101
  Ant tasks, rewriting to
    Gradle tasks 102, 103
application
  running, with Gradle 32, 33
application distributable
  bundling 30
application plugin
  reference link 31
archives 106
artifacts
  publishing 106-108

B

build logic
  applying, to all projects 92-95
  applying, to subprojects 95
  dependency on subproject 96-98
  extracting to buildSrc 129-132
  organizing, in multiproject builds 91
build phases, Gradle
  about 71
  configuration 71, 72
  execution 72
  initialization 71
  life cycle callbacks 73

C

classes, Groovy primer
  about 67
  constructors 67
  instance methods 69
  properties 68
classpath
  JUnit, adding to 24, 25
closure, Groovy 60
code analysis reports 124-126
code coverage 121-124
command-line interface (CLI), Gradle 8-10
compile plugin 51
Continuous Integration (CI) 108-115

D

data structures, Groovy primer
  about 62
  list 62, 63
  maps 64
  set 63
dependency configurations 51
Directed Acyclic Graph (DAG) 72
distribution archive
  building 33, 34
documentation
  about 111
  generating 111, 112
don't repeat yourself (DRY) principle 22

E

enhanced tasks 81
external libraries
  about 48
  dynamic version 49
  transitive dependencies 50

F

first Gradle build script
  about 11, 12
  Gradle Daemon 13
  Gradle Wrapper 14
  task name abbreviation 12

G

Gradle
  about 1, 70
  alternate methods, for installation 5
  application, running with 32, 33
  build phases 71
  command-line interface 8-10
  first build script 11, 12
  installation, verifying 7
  installing 2
  installing, via OS-specific
    package managers 6
  JVM options, setting 7
  manual installation 3
  references 47
Gradle Daemon 13
Gradle distribution
  download link 3
Gradle installation, via OS-specific
  package managers 6
  Linux (Ubuntu) 6
  Mac OS X 6
  Windows 6
Gradle project API
  about 73
  extra properties 76
  project methods 74
  project properties 74, 75
Gradle source code, from GitHub
  reference 56

Gradle Wrapper
  about 14
  build, running via wrapper 14, 15
  wrapper files, generating 14
Gretty
  references 47
Groovy
  about 56
  features 56
  for Gradle build scripts 56
  plugins, applying 69, 70
  references 84
Groovy plugin
  reference 147
Groovy primer
  about 57
  classes 67
  data structures 62
  Groovy code, running 57
  methods 64
  variables 58
Groovy projects
  building 140-144

I

IDE project files
  generating 35
integration testing 119-121

J

Java Development Kit (JDK) 1.6 2
Java plugin
  reference 147
Java Runtime Environment (JRE) 6 2
Java Virtual Machine (JVM) 1
joint compilation 147
JUnit
  adding, to classpath 24, 25
  URL 23

L

lambda 60

M

manual installation, Gradle
  about 3
  on Linux 3
  on Mac OS X 3
  on Windows 4, 5
Maven project, migrating from
  about 103
  common conventions 104
  dependency management 104, 105
  plugin declaration 104
  repositories configuration 105
methods, Groovy primer
  about 64, 65
  calling 65
  default values of parameters 65
  with closure params 67
  with map parameters 66
  with named parameters 66
  with varags 66
multiproject directory layout 87, 88

P

plugin
  about 22, 23, 133, 134
  configuring 136, 137
plugin ID 133
PMD
  URL 122
polyglot application 140
project dependencies
  about 48
  dependency configurations 51, 52
  external libraries 48
  repositories 53
providedCompile plugin 52
providedRuntime plugin 52

Q

Quote of the Day service 140

S

Scala plugin
  reference 147
Scala projects
  building 144-146
Servlet specification 3.1
  reference 37
settings.gradle file 89, 90
simple Java project
  build file, creating 18
  building 17-22
  source files, adding 18, 19
simple Java web project
  artifact, building 42, 43
  build file, creating 41
  building 37
  plugins, using 45-47
  source files, creating 38-40
  web application, running 44, 45
Sonar
  reference 128
source sets 51
specs2
  about 145
  reference 145
System Under Test (SUT) 24

T

task flow control
  about 78
  dependsOn 79
  finalizedBy 79
  mustRunAfter 80
  onlyIf 79
  shouldRunAfter 80
tasks
  about 77
  actions, attaching 78
  creating dynamically 80
  default tasks, setting 81
  enhanced tasks 81
  task flow control 78

task types 81
task types, creating 82, 83
task types, using 82
testCompile plugin 52
TestNG
listener configuration 117
reference 116
test group declaration 117
testing with 115-118
test reports
viewing 26-28
testRuntime plugin 52
tests
fitting, in workflow 28-30
running 25, 26

U

unit testing 23, 119
unit test source
adding 23, 24

V

variables, Groovy primer
about 58
closures 60, 61
regular expressions 60
strings 58, 59

W

workflow
tests, fitting in 28-30

Thank you for buying
Gradle Essentials

About Packt Publishing

Packt, pronounced 'packed', published its first book, *Mastering phpMyAdmin for Effective MySQL Management*, in April 2004, and subsequently continued to specialize in publishing highly focused books on specific technologies and solutions.

Our books and publications share the experiences of your fellow IT professionals in adapting and customizing today's systems, applications, and frameworks. Our solution-based books give you the knowledge and power to customize the software and technologies you're using to get the job done. Packt books are more specific and less general than the IT books you have seen in the past. Our unique business model allows us to bring you more focused information, giving you more of what you need to know, and less of what you don't.

Packt is a modern yet unique publishing company that focuses on producing quality, cutting-edge books for communities of developers, administrators, and newbies alike. For more information, please visit our website at www.packtpub.com.

About Packt Open Source

In 2010, Packt launched two new brands, Packt Open Source and Packt Enterprise, in order to continue its focus on specialization. This book is part of the Packt Open Source brand, home to books published on software built around open source licenses, and offering information to anybody from advanced developers to budding web designers. The Open Source brand also runs Packt's Open Source Royalty Scheme, by which Packt gives a royalty to each open source project about whose software a book is sold.

Writing for Packt

We welcome all inquiries from people who are interested in authoring. Book proposals should be sent to author@packtpub.com. If your book idea is still at an early stage and you would like to discuss it first before writing a formal book proposal, then please contact us; one of our commissioning editors will get in touch with you.

We're not just looking for published authors; if you have strong technical skills but no writing experience, our experienced editors can help you develop a writing career, or simply get some additional reward for your expertise.

Gradle Effective Implementation Guide

ISBN: 978-1-84951-810-9   Paperback: 382 pages

Empower yourself to automate your build

1. Learn the best of Gradle.
2. Work easily with multi-projects.
3. Apply Gradle to your Java, Scala and Groovy projects.

Effective Gradle Implementation [Video]

ISBN: 978-1-78216-766-2   Duration: 03:07 hours

Build, automate, and deploy your application using Gradle

1. Setting up basic and multi-module Java projects.
2. Learn more about the Gradle JavaScript plugin to build your own JavaScript projects.
3. Familiarize yourself with Scala plugin support with available tasks, layout, setup, and dependencies.

Please check **www.PacktPub.com** for information on our titles

Node.js Blueprints

ISBN: 978-1-78328-733-8   Paperback: 268 pages

Develop stunning web and desktop applications with the definitive Node.js

1. Utilize libraries and frameworks to develop real-world applications using Node.js.
2. Explore Node.js compatibility with AngularJS, Socket.io, BackboneJS, EmberJS, and GruntJS.
3. Step-by-step tutorials that will help you to utilize the enormous capabilities of Node.js.

Grails 1.1 Web Application Development

ISBN: 978-1-84719-668-2   Paperback: 328 pages

Reclaiming Productivity for faster Java Web Development

1. Ideal for Java developers new to Groovy and Grails—this book will teach you all you need to create web applications with Grails.
2. Create, develop, test, and deploy a web application in Grails.
3. Take a step further into Web 2.0 using AJAX and the RichUI plug-in in Grails.

Please check www.PacktPub.com for information on our titles

Made in the USA
Monee, IL
17 April 2020